Subjects of Slavery, Agents of Change

SUBJECTS OF SLAVERY,

AGENTS OF CHANGE

Women and Power
in Gothic Novels
and Slave Narratives,
1790–1865

Kari J. Winter

The University of Georgia Press
Athens and London

© 1992 by the University of Georgia Press
Athens, Georgia 30602

Designed by Barbara Henry
Set in 10 on 12 Baskerville by Tseng Information Systems, Inc., with
hand-set display provided by Bowne & Co. Stationers
Printed and bound by Braun-Brumfield
The paper in this book meets the guidelines for permanence
and durability of the Committee on Production Guidelines for
Book Longevity of the Council on Library Resources.

Printed in the United States of America
96 95 94 93 92 C 5 4 3 2 1

Library of Congress Cataloging in Publication Data

Winter, Kari J.
    Subjects of slavery, agents of change : women and power in Gothic
novels and slave narratives, 1790–1865 / Kari J. Winter.
        p.   cm.
    Includes bibliographical references and index.
    ISBN 0-8203-1420-X (alk. paper)
        1. American literature—Women authors—History and criticism.
    2. Slaves—United States—Biography—History and criticism.
    3. English fiction—Women authors—History and criticism.
    4. Slaves' writings, American—History and criticism.   5. Horror
    tales, English—History and criticism.   6. Power (Social sciences) in
    literature.   7. Afro-American women in literature.   8. Gothic
    revival (Literature)   9. Sex role in literature.   10. Women and
    literature.   I. Title.
    PS152.W56   1992
    813'.08729099287—dc20   91-32103
                                                                      CIP

British Library Cataloging in Publication Data available

Emily Dickinson's poem #512 ("The Soul Has Bandaged Moments") is
reprinted by permission of the publishers and the Trustees of Amherst
College from The Poems of Emily Dickinson, Thomas H. Johnson, ed.,
Cambridge, Mass.: The Belknap Press of Harvard University Press,
copyright 1951, 1955, 1979, 1983 by the President and Fellows of
Harvard College.

For my mother,
who taught me the pleasure of learning,
and my father,
who showed me the power of language

The Soul has Bandaged moments—
When too appalled to stir—
She feels some ghastly Fright come up
And stop to look at her—

Salute her—with long fingers—
Caress her freezing hair—
Sip, Goblin, from the very lips
The Lover—hovered—o'er—
Unworthy, that a thought so mean
Accost a Theme—so—fair—

The soul has moments of Escape—
When bursting all the doors—
She dances like a Bomb, abroad,
And swings upon the Hours,

As do the Bee—delirious borne—
Long Dungeoned from his Rose—
Touch Liberty—then know no more,
But Noon, and Paradise—

The Soul's retaken moments—
When, Felon led along,
With shackles on the plumed feet,
And staples, in the Song,

The Horror welcomes her, again,
These, are not brayed of Tongue—

Emily Dickinson

CONTENTS

ACKNOWLEDGMENTS

I AM GRATEFUL to my family, friends, and colleagues for contributing in countless ways to the writing of this book. Discussing feminist theory and Victorian literature with Kathy Retan has stimulated and enhanced my work for the past nine years. Diana Swanson and Jean Martin read sections of the manuscript in its early stages; I appreciate their insight and their friendship. Lydia Schultz, David Waithaka, Steve Fuchs, and Mark Schoenfield were also valuable sources of encouragement and friendship. My brother, John D. Winter, provided financial assistance at an important point. During the final stages of revision, talking with Betty Moss was a constant source of rejuvenation.

This book began as a dissertation. I had the good fortune of working with a wonderful committee at the University of Minnesota; each member enhanced my writing in innumerable ways. Gordon Hirsch stimulated my interest in the eighteenth-century novel and fostered my love of Gothic fiction. Amy Kaminsky provided important encouragement and advice, particularly in areas that address feminist theory. John S. Wright was an invaluable source of information on African American literature and theory; I could not have undertaken this comparative study without his encouragement, insight, and inspiration. Toni McNaron's strength and wisdom as a feminist critic were another constant source of inspiration; her support gave me the courage to pursue my interests, no matter how risky they seemed at the time. And Michael Hancher was an exemplary adviser: a kind, intelligent teacher throughout my years in graduate school and an extraordinarily careful reader and critic. He commented extensively on multiple drafts of the manuscript and helped to refine the style, language, and logic throughout. The remaining errors are, of course, all my own.

I am grateful to the National Endowment for the Humanities for enabling me to attend a summer seminar in 1991, "The Slave Narrative Tradition in African American Literature," directed by William L.

Andrews. My arguments were sharpened on many points by the discussions we all had, as a group and one-on-one. I am particularly indebted to William L. Andrews, John Sekora, and Laura Quinn for their encouraging, helpful comments on the manuscript. Amy Southerland generously assisted me with several last-minute research and editing tasks.

I am also grateful to Dana D. Nelson and Lucinda H. MacKethan, whose enthusiastic comments on the manuscript enriched my work. Everyone at the University of Georgia Press was a pleasure to work with, especially my editor, Nancy Grayson Holmes.

INTRODUCTION

WOMEN
AND
SLAVERY

I N 1700 the English essayist Mary Astell asked, "If *all Men are born free,* how is it that all Women are born Slaves? As they must be, if the being subjected to the *inconstant, uncertain, unknown, arbitrary Will* of Men, be the *perfect Condition of Slavery?*" (107). Astell persistently attacked the patriarchal family as a tyrannical institution that enslaved women, and she vehemently protested against women's exclusion from institutions of education. Her controversial views attracted a substantial number of readers; indeed, her books "ran to several editions in her lifetime" (Hill 2).[1]

Echoing Astell in the 1790s, Mary Wollstonecraft asked in the opening chapter of her Gothic novel *The Wrongs of Woman*: "[Is] not the world a vast prison, and women born slaves?" (79). Throughout her work, Wollstonecraft argued that children's "slavish bondage to parents cramps every faculty of the mind" and that when girls in particular are "kept down by their parents . . . and thus taught slavishly to submit to their parents, they are prepared for the slavery of marriage" (*A Vindication* 155). As a theist who rejected much of Christianity, Wollstonecraft was able to attack systematically both the institution of marriage and the structure of the patriarchal family without being paralyzed by religious scruples. However, she still faced an ancient tradition of secular ideas and laws regarding women's "natural" inferiority and subservience. The subjection of women was rarely disguised or subterranean in Western culture before the eighteenth century; Graeco-Roman laws "enforced the principles of women as 'in-house slaves'" and church fathers and legislators repeatedly reenforced the same principles (Sekora, *Luxury* 59).[2]

The ancient world's economy was "founded upon slavery and other forms of involuntary servitude"; therefore, the main function of Greek and Roman law was "to ensure that the great majority of persons remained dependent and continued to perform the essential and involuntary labor that sustained the legislators' independence" (Sekora, *Luxury* 54). Aristotle articulated the ideology that has dominated Western thought and law for millennia when he argued that

> for all tame animals there is an advantage in being under human control, as this secures their survival. And as regards the relationship between male and female, the former is naturally superior, the latter naturally inferior, the former rules and the latter is subject.
>
> By analogy, the same must necessarily apply to mankind as a whole. Therefore all men who differ from one another by as much as the soul differs from the body or man from a wild beast (and that is the state of those who work by using their bodies, and for whom that is the best they can do)—these people are slaves by nature, and it is better for them to be subject to this kind of control, as it is better for the other creatures I have mentioned. For a man who is able to belong to another person is by nature a slave (for that is why he belongs to someone else). (*Politics* 1.5)

For Aristotle, women are slaves, slaves are like women, and both are like domestic animals. He begins by suggesting that the primary social hierarchy, on which subsequent distinctions are based, is the subordination of the female to the male, but ultimately he shows that the oppositions of male-female and free-slave are reciprocally interdependent. I would argue that, because of this fundamental interdependence, the oppression of women and male slaves can be understood fully only when the ideology of male domination is examined in conjunction with the ideology of slavery.

In the hands of feminists like Astell and Wollstonecraft, the ancient misogynist rhetoric comparing women to slaves was turned back against the claims of patriarchal ideology.[3] During the nineteenth century, the comparison of women to slaves became pervasive in British and American women's writing and in the writings of progressive men like John Stuart Mill and Frederick Douglass. In particular, female Gothic novelists in Britain and feminist-abolitionists in the United States represented imprisonment and slavery as the central paradigms of woman's condition in patriarchal society. More than any other literary genres of the period, the female Gothic and slave narrative genres focused on the terrifying injustices at the foundation of the Western social order.

Between 1790 and 1830—the period when Gothic narratives dominated popular fiction in England—a "a full-fledged slave system" emerged in the southern United States (Patterson 73). This system of exploitation was based primarily on race and secondarily on gender. As Eugene Genovese has shown, American slaveholders and slaves "did not fail to see the connection between their masters' patriarchal stance toward their wives and children and that toward their slaves" (74). Seargent S. Prentiss, for example, introduced "a resolution in [the Mississippi] state legislature in 1836 that declared: 'We hold discussions upon the subject [slavery] as equally impertinent with discussion upon our relations, wives, and children'" (Genovese 74). Countless male slaveholders compared themselves to Biblical patriarchs and argued, in the words of one slaveholder, that "all men are born dependant [*sic*]. . . . More than one-half the human race in fact, and at least one-fifth slaves in name."[4] Most feminists concurred with this classic patriarchal description of society, with one crucial difference: what slaveholders labeled "nature," feminists named "oppression."

Since the civil rights movement of the 1960s, many literary scholars have examined representations of slavery and race in the texts of nineteenth-century white American writers, but they have largely ignored British involvement in formulating racist ideology.[5] British men of letters, like the general British population, were divided on the slavery issue. For example, Samuel Johnson was "bitterly hostile" towards slavery, but his usually loyal disciple, James Boswell, supported it (Ragatz 243). Most eighteenth-century male Gothic novelists supported slavery; indeed, William Beckford was an active representative of the interests of Caribbean slaveholders in the British Parliament, and M. G. Lewis was an absentee owner of West Indian slaves. Physical distance did not make British slaveholders any less responsible for slavery than American slaveholders; in fact, "absenteeism was an unmitigated disaster for slaves insofar as their material treatment was concerned" (Patterson 423n33).

In contrast to male Gothic novelists, most feminist writers in England and the United States saw the enslavement of African peoples as a brutal case of human oppression that was fundamentally connected to the oppression of white women. In America the feminist-abolitionist Angelina Grimké stated: "The investigation of the rights of the slave has led me to a better understanding of my own" (114). She argued that the human rights of black men, women, and the working classes were all intertwined; therefore, the nation was "in a death-struggle. It must either become one vast slaveocracy of petty tyrants, or wholly the land of the free" (qtd. in A. Davis 68).

Few nineteenth-century white feminists could match Grimké's comprehensive social analysis; indeed, as twentieth-century black feminists (including Angela Davis, Bell Hooks, and Hazel Carby) have repeatedly shown, since the eighteenth century many white feminists have reproduced white supremacism in their work. Nonetheless, significant numbers of white abolitionist-feminists regarded the enslavement of black women as an attack on all womankind. For them, the experiences of women like Harriet Jacobs "dramatized the feminist analysis of the parallel slavery of race and sex. Thus her career furnished strong support for the antebellum feminist argument that chattel slavery was only the most egregious manifestation of the tyranny of patriarchal power in America. . . . For two decades Angelina Grimké had been referring to politically silent women in the free states as 'the white slaves of the North'; by 1857 Elizabeth Cady Stanton had denounced the unequal status of the wife in marriage as 'nothing more nor less than legalized prostitution'" (Andrews, *To Tell* 247). The social analyses of Angelina and Sarah Grimké and Elizabeth Cady Stanton placed them squarely in the tradition of English feminists like Mary Wollstonecraft, who certainly would have agreed that Jacobs's enslavement was representative of woman's condition under patriarchy.

Throughout the nineteenth century in both Britain and the United States, white middle-class feminist analyses of women's oppression, articulated in essays and dramatized in novels, short stories, and poems, focused on three areas: marriage, education, and (to a lesser extent) the franchise. First, the institution of marriage was represented as the mainstay of women's subjugation because marriage "not only gave the husband legal ownership of his wife's person, property, and issue, it was indissoluble, except that an influential man could obtain a divorce by act of Parliament" (Sunstein 12). The institution of marriage permanently prevented the autonomy of women, denied women control of their own sexuality, and mandated women's economic dependence.

Second, British and American feminists argued that the dominant ideology perpetuated itself by denying useful knowledge to all people other than the white men in the ruling classes. Led by Wollstonecraft, many women writers asserted that access to knowledge and mastery of language were the primary tools by which women could liberate their minds from patriarchal ideology. Third, lack of access to the vote represented to many women their complete social disempowerment. Gaining the vote meant empowering themselves to implement women's liberation. Various groups of feminists disagreed sharply over which of these three issues should receive priority, but throughout the century marriage, education, and the franchise remained pressing issues for white feminists.

Important as these issues were, did they justify drawing analogies between women's oppression and slavery? Bell Hooks has criticized the comparison: "Theoretically, the white woman's legal status under patriarchy may have been that of 'property,' but she was in no way subjected to the de-humanization and brutal oppression that was the lot of the slave. When white reformers made synonymous the impact of sexism on their lives, they were not revealing an awareness or sensitivity to the slave's lot; they were simply appropriating the horror of the slave experience to enhance their own cause" (126). Hooks certainly is right in maintaining that the material deprivation and physical abuse inflicted upon American slaves were far more severe than the forms of oppression generally inflicted upon white middle-class American and British women. Furthermore, white women (feminist and non-feminist) often increased the sufferings of black slaves by exploiting and abusing them in multiple ways.

However, as I discussed above, the association of the status of women with that of slaves is older than feminism; it was first made in ancient texts written by men in positions of power. Furthermore, slavery cannot be defined solely in terms of brutality of oppression. In fact, Eugene Genovese has shown that often the slaves who had the least access to freedom were allowed to live in relative material comfort, as the slaveholders attempted to reconcile them to a permanent state of subjugation.[6] When "free" women called themselves slaves they were not equating their physical sufferings with the sufferings of American slaves. Rather, they were describing the social ordering of power whereby women are kept in a perpetual state of subjection to physical, emotional, and economic exploitation by men. Fighting against slavery helped white women to better understand the dynamics of all human oppression. Angelina Grimké found "the Anti-Slavery cause to be the high school of morals in our land—the school in which *human rights* are more fully investigated, and better understood and taught, than in any other. Here a great fundamental principle is uplifted and illuminated, and from this central light, rays innumerable stream all around" (114).

American slavery was in many ways an atypical form which depended on a peculiar mixture of Western colonialist ideology, racism, and economic demands. Long after African Americans were declared free in law, they remained enslaved in social practice—subjected to severe racial violence and economic exploitation. In 1903 W. E. B. Du Bois observed, "This much all men know: despite compromise, war, and struggle, the Negro is not free. In the backwoods of the Gulf States, for miles and miles, he may not leave the plantation of his birth; in well-nigh the whole rural South the black farmers are peons, bound by law and custom to an economic slavery, from which the only escape is death or the penitentiary. In the most cultured sections and cities of the South the Negroes are a segregated servile caste, with restricted rights and privileges" (29). Many African Americans believed that their lives were more brutal and more hopeless after "Emancipation" than before.[7]

It should be clear, then, that "slavery" and "freedom" are interdependent and problematic concepts. As Orlando Patterson and Catherine Gallagher have shown, questions about slavery lead inevitably to questions about freedom. Patterson points out that "slavery is associated not only with the development of advanced economies, but also with the emergence of several of the most profoundly cherished ideals and beliefs in the Western tradition. The idea of freedom and the concept of property were both intimately bound up with the rise of slavery, their very antithesis" (viii). The dominant ideology in every culture mystifies that culture's particular forms of domination; indeed, Barthes suggests that such mystification is the primary function of ideology (121). To prevent power imbalances from being recognized as oppressive, the dominant ideology represents the existing power hierarchy as ordained by God and nature.

In all patriarchal cultures, the freedom of the patriarch depends on the denial of freedom to women. Patriarchal ideology attempts to naturalize that power imbalance by "transform[ing] history into nature," thereby disguising men's responsibility for the oppression they create (Barthes 129, 151). Thus, although "Plato and Aristotle and the great Roman jurists . . . recogniz[ed] the necessary correlation between their love of their own freedom and its denial to others," they argued that their social system was based on nature (Patterson viii–ix). To reiterate Aristotle's words quoted above, women are "*naturally* inferior. . . . [some] people are slaves *by nature*. . . . For a man who is able to belong to another person is *by nature* a slave (for that is why he belongs to someone else)" (my emphasis). Aristotle's circular logic (whatever is, is natural and it is natural because it is) ensures that there will be no alternative to the status quo.

Like slavery and racism, the oppression of women has assumed different forms in different historical eras. Identifying the basic elements of slavery as it has been practiced throughout history may enable us to see beyond some of Western culture's ideological mystifications. Furthermore, defining slavery historically is necessary to illuminate the feminist assertion that women are born slaves in a patriarchal culture.

In 1900, exactly two hundred years after Mary Astell compared women to slaves, the Dutch scholar H. J. Nieboer published an influential definition of slavery based on an ambitious comparative study of what he called "the phenomena of savage life" (vii). His book, *Slavery as an Industrial System: Ethnographical Researches* (expanded in 1910), established him as the "greatest name in the comparative history of slavery" until the 1980s, in the opinion of many historians and sociologists (Banton 947). His interpretation of slavery as "a mode of organizing labour" has remained a prevalent view (Banton 947). However, I see Nieboer's work as informative primarily because his use of "science" illuminates the ways patriarchal, white supremacist ideology often has been reproduced in scholarly texts.

In his first chapter, Nieboer attempts to define slavery by distinguishing it from the condition of women. He protests against the "careless" and "inaccurate" application of the term "slavery" to "the so-called 'Subjection of Women'" (4). He is forced, however, to analyze the apparent enslavement of women in some detail because the nineteenth-century male ethnographers on whose research he relied repeatedly (if grudgingly) described women as enslaved in "savage" cultures. Ironically, Nieboer's attempt to refute this idea provides so much support for the feminist argument that I will summarize his points in detail, keeping his emphases. His rhetorical strategy is to describe the arguments of "the advocates of women's rights," including "some ethnographers and theorists," and then belittle them:

A. Research shows: *"The wife is acquired by the husband without her consent being asked"* (11). Nieboer's rebuttal: "In some cases we are told, that *the girl's wishes* are to some extent *taken into consideration* as to the choice of her husband" (17).

B. Research shows: *"The wife is entirely in the power of her husband, and treated accordingly"* (12). Specifically, studies show: (a) wives are often called slaves; (b) women are treated with contempt; (c) wives are routinely beaten, tortured, mutilated, killed, and even eaten by their husbands; (d) wives are exchanged between male friends, lent to other men, prostituted, and sold; (e) widows become the property of their late husbands' brothers (12–14). Nieboer's rebuttal: "Sometimes the ethnographers tell of much *affection* existing between husband and wife. . . . *The husband does not always enjoy such an entire freedom of action towards his wife.* Sometimes, for punishing and divorcing her, *he must have the consent of the tribe*" (18–19). "We even find cases of *the wife putting a check upon her husband*"—sometimes she assumes "*a real as-cendancy*" over him (20). "*Exchange of wives* does not seem always to take place against their will"—women often "prostitute themselves" and they are "honored" by the attentions of "men of a superior race" (20–21).

C. Research shows: "*The husband makes his wife work for him*" (15). Specific studies document that, under the constant threat of violence, wives build habitations, transport property, care for children, plant crops, fish, hunt, collect fuel and water, and cook. They work unceas-ingly and with little reward (15–16). Nieboer's rebuttal: Although men appear to lead "an easy and idle existence," in fact they often work. Also, we must not forget that they "protect" their families (23).

The evidence that Nieboer cites clearly documents that women were enslaved in many "savage" cultures throughout the world; his weak rebuttals are obviously based on misogynist assumptions. He finally concedes that, in "savage" societies, the wife *is* "the property of her husband" and a "forced labourer" (24). He still insists, however, that women cannot be seen as slaves. His clinching argument is that women are, after all, *women*. They cannot be slaves because "besides being forced labourers they are wives; hence it follows that their relation towards their husbands is wholly bound up with the sexual and family life: it is their character as women, not as labourers, that prevails" (24). His immersion in patriarchal ideology blinds him to the ludicrous illogic with which he concludes his argument: "*Slavery proper does not exist, when there are none but female slaves.* For when females only are enslaved, the reason probably is, that they are valued as women, not only as labourers" (25). Like Aristotle, Neiboer employs an ideological, essentialist concept of "nature" to justify men's subjugation of women, even going so far as to equate enslaving women with "valuing" them.

In 1982, Orlando Patterson, professor of sociology at Harvard, pub-lished a monumental book entitled *Slavery and Social Death: A Compara-tive Study.* This book broke new ground by defining slavery as a means of organizing *power* rather than labor. Although Patterson devotes little attention to the subjection of nominally "free" women, his comprehensive and convincing analysis of slavery as a relation of domination greatly illuminates the condition of all women in patriarchal cultures. He discredits Nieboer's definition of slavery as a mode of organizing (men's) labor by showing that in many societies slaves produced virtually nothing—they often were, in fact, economically dependent on the master. Drawing on Marx's analysis of different forms of power, Patterson defines a "personalistic" and a "materialistic" idiom of power (18). In personalistic societies, "power relations are not mystified" (19); everyone understands that slaves are acquired to enhance the power and honor of the master. In materialistic societies, relations of subjection and dependence are disguised; the "power relationship is no longer viewed as power over persons but as power over commodities" (19). In other words, capitalistic ideology requires slaveholders to view slavery as a system based on maximizing profit, not power. The "fetishism of commodities" obscures "the basic power relationship" (19).

In contrast to Nieboer, who limited his research to "savage" societies, Patterson analyzes the institution of slavery as it has been practiced globally throughout history. He begins by noting that although antebellum Americans referred to slavery as "the peculiar institution," there is "nothing notably peculiar about the institution of slavery. It has existed from before the dawn of human history right down to the twentieth century, in the most primitive of human societies and in the most civilized" (vii). Patterson shows that the purposes for which human beings have been enslaved and the material conditions they have experienced have varied widely. What then constitutes slavery? He argues that slavery is a relation of domination that has three "constituent elements." First, although "all human relationships are structured and defined by the relative power of the interacting persons" (1), slavery is unusual in "the extremity of power involved, and all that immediately implies, and in the qualities of coercion that brought the relation into being and sustained it" (2). Slave ideology attempted to eradicate the autonomous existence of the slave; as one slaveholder put it, "Without the master the slave does not exist, and he is socializable only through his master" (4). Furthermore, "The most distinctive attribute of the slave's powerlessness was that it always originated (or was conceived of as having originated) as a substitute for death, usually violent death" (5). However they were enslaved, whether captured in war, rescued from natural calamity, sold into slavery, or born into it, slaves were literally or symbolically sentenced to death by their enslavers. Resisting enslavement meant death; the slave's "execution was suspended only as long as the slave acquiesced in his powerlessness" (5). In other words, slaves could maintain physical life only by accepting their social death.

Second, slavery is marked by "the slave's natal alienation," a sign of his social death: "Alienated from all 'rights' or claims of birth, [the slave] ceased to belong in his own right to any legitimate social order. . . . Not only was the slave denied all claims on, and obligations to, his parents and living blood relations but, by extension, all such claims and obligations on his more remote ancestors and on his descendants. He was truly a genealogical isolate" (5). Although slaves "in both ancient and modern times had strong social ties among themselves, . . . these relationships were never recognized as binding" by the dominant society (6).

Third, slavery is universally characterized by the master's sense of his own honor, which depends on his view of slaves as dishonored. According to slaveholders' ideology, "the slave could have no honor because of the origin of his status, the indignity and all-pervasiveness of his indebtedness, his absence of any independent social existence, but most of all because he was without power except through another" (10). In sum, then, Patterson defines slavery as *the permanent, violent domination of natally alienated and generally dishonored persons*" (13).

Although eighteenth- and nineteenth-century white feminists did not develop a systematic, comprehensive definition of women's slavery, there are striking parallels between Patterson's definition and feminist analyses of women's condition. First, feminists have shown repeatedly that in patriarchal cultures women are perpetually and violently *dominated* by men.[8] Second, like slaves throughout history, women often have been defined as *socially dead:* persons who do not exist except in relation to fathers, husbands, or brothers. Laws forbidding women to own property, to control money, or to witness in court indicate the legal denial of women's independent existence. Third, women live in a condition of *general dishonor* in patriarchal cultures, despite mystifications of women's status such as the Victorian ideology of the angel in the house and the southern cult of true womanhood. Patriarchal ideology is absolutely dependent on the construction of a fundamental male-female opposition. Just as freedom historically derived its meaning in opposition to slavery, masculinity derived its meaning in opposition to femininity. To be a man, that most honorific and desirable of all states of being, is *not* to be a woman.

Patterson points to the similarities between the condition of slaves and the condition of at least some women when he states that "it was easy for men in most precapitalist societies to identify the status of a female slave with that of free concubine or junior wife. The difference in status usually had no material consequences for the woman, although it did for her children" (228). The fact that the difference in status between enslaved and "free" women often had material consequences for their children illuminates one of the differences between the oppression of "free" women in general and the oppression of slaves: "free" women are not usually "natally alienated," in Patterson's sense. In other words, nominally free women usually possess socially recognized relationships with their families—their living relatives and their ancestors. As Patterson shows, these family connections are of enormous importance to one's social existence; genealogical isolates are socially nonexistent.

Although "free" women are not literally "natally alienated," women writers often represent themselves and/or their heroines as genealogical isolates on a symbolic level. As Northrop Frye has shown, protagonists in Romance are often solitary orphans, uninformed or misinformed about their absent or dead parents.[9] Women writers—particularly female Gothic novelists—usually attach a special significance to the heroine's isolation and depict the absence of *mothers* as particularly devastating, perhaps because they fear that daughters, like mothers, are destined to be "utterly annihilated."[10]

The social alienation of nineteenth-century British novelists and their heroines was never as complete as the alienation of African peoples who were forcibly removed from their homelands, shipped overseas under brutal conditions, and auctioned off as chattel in the Americas. Nor were Gothic authors and their heroines terrorized to the degree that black slaves were when they were subjected to the perpetual threat (and frequent reality) of being sold apart from their families. Yet both women's Gothic novels and slave narratives lament their protagonists' isolation and alienation, and both genres emphasize women's attempts to maintain human connections.

Patterson identifies two ways in which slaveholding societies conceived of slaves' alienation; he names them the *intrusive* and *extrusive* modes of representing social death. This distinction illuminates some of the differences between the typical form of "free" women's oppression and the specific form of American enslavement of Africans. In the intrusive conception, slaves are represented as intruders from "a hostile, alien culture," "strangers in a strange land" disconnected from any ancestral myth. In the extrusive conception, "the dominant image of the slave was that of an insider who had fallen, one who ceased to belong and had been expelled from normal participation in the community because of a failure to meet certain minimal legal or socioeconomic norms of behavior" (41). Obviously the social death of Africans enslaved in America was represented in the intrusive mode. Patriarchal representations of "free" women resemble the extrusive mode of representing social death; "free" women are typically represented as fallen, innately inferior beings.

In summary, then, Patterson's definition of slavery fits remarkably well with the general condition of women as represented in the texts of many women, both slave and "free."

However, we cannot overlook the fact that white middle-class women in England and black ex-slave women in America lived through and wrote about significantly different experiences. Gothic novels were published and marketed for a burgeoning audience of predominantly middle-class women readers. The novels were not only works of fiction; they were Romances, in Hawthorne's sense. Because the Gothic genre was distinguished by its free use of imagination, female novelists found it to be a particularly adaptable mode for covertly exploring sexual politics. Throughout the eighteenth and nineteenth centuries, the legal status and economic roles of women in Britain were in a state of flux. Identifying how women were oppressed was not an easy task; writers were confused by the contradictory, volatile mystifications of women's condition. While American slavery was unmistakably identified as slavery, the oppression of white women had become in many ways disguised and subterranean. Female Gothic writers developed a genre that was particularly well suited to the historical situation; the main task of the Gothic heroine is to uncover and name the horrors that fill her world.

Unlike Gothic novels, slave narratives were written for an explicit and immediate political purpose—the abolition of slavery. They usually were published and marketed by abolitionists as political propaganda. For reasons examined in chapter 1, slave narratives comprise a genre that is less clearly defined and more critically neglected than the female Gothic genre. While many female Gothic novels have been readily available for decades, most of the slave narratives written by women before the Civil War were not republished until the 1980s. This book focuses throughout on texts written by women, but the paucity of criticism on slave narratives as well as the fact that relatively few women's narratives were written or survived has led me to supplement my readings of women's slave narratives in two noteworthy ways. First, I often use slave narratives written by men to contextualize and to expand my discussion of central ideas in women's narratives. Second, I sometimes turn to twentieth-century African American women's novels that employ the slave narrative tradition, because writers like Zora Neale Hurston and Toni Morrison often write their best literary theory in the form of fiction. In particular, I know of no work that reconstructs and illuminates both the female Gothic and the slave narrative traditions better than *Beloved.*

Despite their differences, both genres of prose narrative appealed to wide audiences before 1865.[11] Analyzing the popular appeal of women's literature, Julia Kristeva suggests that literature often functions for female writers and readers as a mode of self-affirmation and protest against the dominant order. She asks, "Why literature? Is it because, faced with social norms, literature reveals a certain knowledge and sometimes the truth itself about an otherwise repressed, nocturnal, secret, and unconscious universe? Because it thus redoubles the social contract by exposing the unsaid, the uncanny? And because it makes a game, a space of fantasy and pleasure, out of the abstract and frustrating order of social signs, the words of everyday communication?" (31). Despite the substantial differences between female Gothic novels and slave narratives (the former is encoded as "fantasy and pleasure" and the latter as "politics and propaganda"), both genres do indeed expose "repressed, nocturnal, secret, and unconscious" truths about the patriarchal world. Both genres focus on the sexual politics at the heart of patriarchal culture, and both represent the terrifying aspects of life for women in a patriarchal culture. Furthermore, the two genres are remarkably similar in imagery, structure, and social analysis. Nineteenth-century black women's narratives both complement and challenge the social analyses articulated in white women's Gothic novels because they combine strident attacks on the patriarchal order with incisive critiques of white women's racism and classism. Analyzing female Gothic novels and slave narratives across lines of genre, discipline, class, and race illuminates the ideological work being done in each text.

In this book I read both genres as sites of ideological struggle. All narratives are shaped to a large extent by the material conditions in which they are produced, but they are also (in Fredric Jameson's phrase) agents in "the elaboration, reproduction, or critique of ideology" (45). My central concern is to examine how female Gothic novels and slave narratives engaged the dominant classist, racist, patriarchal discourse and created possibilities for new, feminist ways of thinking.[12]

IN a poem that mirrors the structure of most female Gothic novels and slave narratives, Emily Dickinson dramatizes a movement from imprisonment to escape to recapture. She begins the poem (#512) with a description of the dreadful moment when a woman confronts the "ghastly Fright" of her world:

> The Soul has Bandaged moments—
> When too appalled to stir—
> She feels some ghastly Fright come up
> And stop to look at her—
>
> Salute her—with long fingers—
> Caress her freezing hair—
> Sip, Goblin, from the very lips
> The Lover—hovered—o'er—
> Unworthy, that a thought so mean
> Accost a theme—so—fair

Gothic novels and slave narratives written by women focus on the "Bandaged moments" of life, the moments of pain and terror. In these moments, even the "fair themes" of paternalistic ideology prove "unworthy" and coercive. The "Lover" is unmasked as a "Goblin" and acts of "love" are recognized as acts of terror. The bandages that bind the soul are not instruments of healing; rather, they are bonds of constriction similar to the garments of a mummy or the straitjackets that paralyze the "insane." Dickinson, like Gothic novelists and slave narrators, associates "Bandaged moments" with death: "freezing" is the soul's response to the "Goblin" that accosts her.

Women's Gothic novels and slave narratives also contain "moments of escape" when the soul touches "Liberty" and envisions a world beyond patriarchy. In Dickinson's words:

> The soul has moments of Escape—
> When bursting all the doors—
> She dances like a Bomb, abroad,
> And swings upon the Hours,

As do the Bee—delirious borne—
Long Dungeoned from his Rose—
Touch Liberty—then know no more,
But Noon, and Paradise—

The image of the soul dancing "like a Bomb, abroad," suggests that the moments of escape are powerful and exhilarating but dangerous. The danger is that the soul's explosive energy may lead to self-destruction; the hope, of course, is that her energy will be directed towards self-assertion and against the "ghastly Fright" that threatens to annihilate her. The image of the soul "swing[ing] upon the Hours" expresses a sense of time liberated from linear movement. Perpetual "Noon, and Paradise" replace the tedious passage of time in a dungeon.

For Dickinson, as for female Gothic novelists and slave narrators, simply "touch[ing] Liberty" intoxicates the long-imprisoned soul. However, her moments of escape do not last—she is soon recaptured and reimprisoned:

The Soul's retaken moments—
When, Felon led along,
With shackles on the plumed feet,
And staples, in the Song,

The Horror welcomes her, again,
These, are not brayed of Tongue—

This poem captures precisely the tone of women's Gothic novels and slave narratives. Feelings of horror dominate, punctuated by brief moments of exhilaration and freedom. These moments are essential to female survival and are the birthplace of feminist activity, even though they are followed by times of constriction ("shackles on the plumed feet"), repression ("staples, in the Song"), and silence ("These, are not brayed of Tongue").

Chapter 1 of this book examines the critical treatment that Gothic novels and slave narratives have received and the ways in which the authors fought to break silences. While female Gothic novels have been patronized as sentimental, popular (sub)literature, slave narratives have been seen as raw historical material that the credentialed scholar may use or ignore, as he sees fit. Located at the extremes of fantasy and history, then, women's Gothic narratives and slave narratives have, until recently, been denied serious critical attention. Significantly, the social critique in these marginalized texts always begins with a representation of oppressed protagonists struggling to find a voice and an audience.

After chapter 1, this book follows the structure of Dickinson's poem. I move from an analysis of the authors' representations of the horrors of patriarchy (chapter 2) to an examination of their representations of possibilities of resistance and escape (chapters 3 and 4). I conclude with an exploration of the authors' difficulties in closing their texts. On the one hand, the classic final chapters of slave narratives and female Gothic novels assure readers that the former slave is "free at last" and that the Gothic heroine is "hastening to perfect felicity." On the other hand, the protagonist's freedom is always qualified, often so much that the text returns, as Dickinson predicts, to constriction, repression, and silence.

1
BREAKING
SILENCE

Women's stories have not been told. And without stories there is no articulation of experience. Without stories a woman is lost when she comes to make the important decisions of her life. She does not learn to value her struggles, to celebrate her strengths, to comprehend her pain. Without stories she cannot understand herself. Without stories she is alienated from those deeper experiences of self and world that have been called spiritual or religious. She is closed in silence.

Carol Christ, *Diving Deep and Surfacing*

Women have often felt insane when cleaving to the truth of our experience. Our future depends on the sanity of each of us, and we have a profound stake, beyond the personal, in the project of describing our reality as candidly and fully as we can to each other.

Adrienne Rich, "Women and Honor: Some Notes on Lying"

HE WOMEN'S MOVEMENT in Britain and America was revitalized in the late 1960s by women who began to break silences about their experiences of exploitation at home, at school, at work, and in bed. As these women shared their stories with each other in consciousness-raising groups, they discovered two fundamental feminist insights. First, the personal is political. Second, power is intricately bound to language. Because patriarchal domination is enacted and maintained in language, when a woman claims a voice, she claims power.

As women of the 1970s and 1980s began to claim our voices, we also began to hear stories from the past. We discovered that Carol Christ's assertion that "women's stories have not been told" is not quite accurate. Women *have* told their stories in one form or another throughout history, but most of their stories have been belittled, ignored, or lost. Their creative expressions have rarely been recognized as art. Those women who have tried to "tell all the truth" have often been forced to "tell it slant," as Emily Dickinson put it. When attempting to tell our own stories, we discovered, in the words of Mikhail Bakhtin, that "language is not a neutral medium that passes freely and easily into the private property of the speaker's intentions; it is populated—over-populated—with the intentions of others. Expropriating it, forcing it to submit to one's own intentions and accents, is a difficult and complicated process" (294). Examining the ways women writers engaged the ideological systems that attempted to silence them between 1790 and 1865 illuminates ways that we who are still fighting for liberation may expropriate language for our own purposes.

In *The Political Unconscious: Narrative as a Socially Symbolic Act*, Fredric Jameson observes that "we never really confront a text immediately, in all its freshness as a thing-in-itself. Rather, texts come before us as the always-already read; we apprehend them through sedimented layers of previous interpretations, or—if the text is brand-new—through the sedimented reading habits and categories developed by those inherited interpretive traditions" (9). Within the literary academy, "sedimented layers" of interpretation have belittled women's Gothic fiction and ignored women's slave narratives. Feminist literary critics interested in these genres must work both to liberate the texts from "inherited [white supremacist, masculinist] interpretive traditions" and to develop *new* "reading habits and categories."

SEXUAL/TEXTUAL POLITICS OF TERROR

Writers of Gothic fiction were often called "terrorists" in the eighteenth century, but did their texts reveal (in Kristeva's phrase) "the terror of power or the power of terrorism"? In other words, how did Gothic writers position themselves in relation to the dominant power structure? The texts written by male and female Gothic novelists and the critical treatment these texts have received since their publication suggest that men and women not only pick up the pen from very different cultural positions—they usually employ the pen to very different ends.

The publication of Horace Walpole's *The Castle of Otranto* in 1764 conventionally marks the beginning of Gothic literature. Although Walpole's themes, sensibilities, and supernatural devices had predecessors in Jacobean theater and the "grave-yard" poetry of the early eighteenth century, *The Castle of Otranto* began a new tradition of prose fiction. The plots of Gothic novels do not depend on comedy or tragedy but rather on suspense, anxiety, and fear. Kate Ferguson Ellis has argued that Gothic novels "can be distinguished by the presence of houses in which people are locked in and locked out. They are concerned with violence done to familial bonds that is frequently directed against women" (3). To be more specific, distinctive features of Gothic fiction include decaying castles, bleeding ghosts, family secrets, mysterious crimes, sexual violence, confused wandering or desperate fleeing through dark streets, labyrinths, caves, tunnels, turrets and graveyards, and surrealistic journeys over sublime landscapes.[1] Together these features create a nightmarish atmosphere, intense emotional involvement, a sense of a mythic return to the origins of life (the mysteries of sexuality and the mother's womb), and a primal conflict between good and evil.

Like Romantic poetry, Gothic fiction characteristically represents boundaries between self and other, psyche and world as remarkably fluid. This fluidity of boundaries is expressed in the instability of individual identities and the common device of narrative frames in which the central themes and plots of the novel occur repeatedly through subplots. Sophia Lee's *The Recess* (1783–85) and Charles Maturin's *Melmoth the Wanderer* (1820) are extreme examples of the seemingly endless repetition that Gothic novelists sometimes achieved.

The Castle of Otranto has served novelists and moviemakers for two centuries as a stockroom full of props. From 1764 until the 1790s, dozens of writers experimented with this new form of fiction; in the 1790s Gothic fiction came of age with the publication of novels by Ann Radcliffe and M. G. Lewis. The Gothic genre has proven remarkably fertile; its descendants include detective fiction, science fiction, apocalyptic fiction, ghost stories, and horror stories, genres that are central to television and film in the twentieth century.[2]

Traditional critics of Gothic fiction have focused their attention on Gothic novels by men, either ignoring the existence of Gothic fiction by women or overlooking themes that were central to female writers but of little interest to male writers. In the 1930s Mario Praz's remarkable book *The Romantic Agony* provided hundreds of examples of necrophilia, sadism, racism, mutilation of women, cannibalism, rape, vampirism, incest, murder, self-flagellation, degradations, and desecrations in Gothic and Romantic texts. Praz argues convincingly that perverse themes are characteristic of Gothic and Romantic literature, and the evidence he marshals can be very useful for the feminist critic who is attempting to understand the male Gothic and Romantic tradition. However, Praz takes virtually all of his examples from men's texts; he fails to notice that women created a different tradition. He assumes that "as the literary tradition has been the monopoly of man, at any rate up till the present, it is natural that women writers should slavishly adopt in their works the masculine point of view" (113). He repeats a common patriarchal theme when he asserts that women are, at best, passive receptacles of men's ideas. For example, he dismisses the author of *Frankenstein* with the comment that "all Mrs. Shelley did was to provide a passive reflection of some of the wild fantasies which, as it were, hung in the air about her" (114).[3]

In the 1970s Tzvetan Todorov argued that fantastic literature (which includes the Gothic) establishes "an equivalence . . . between sexual love and death" and that "the transformation of an attractive woman into a corpse is the pattern, repeated time and again" (*Fantastic* 135–36). Todorov's analyses are insightful but, like Praz, he focuses almost exclusively on men's writing. Elizabeth Napier's 1987 study, *The Failure of the Gothic*, shares the prevalent practice of making generic claims about the Gothic without taking into account the work of women writers. Napier endorses "Coleridge's charge of moral and aesthetic trifling" in Gothic literature, arguing that the Gothic demonstrates "a complex inability to confront both moral and aesthetic responsibilities; its often feverish search after sensation is puzzlingly joined with a deliberate retreat from meaning" (1, 39). Rather than increasing the reader's moral sensitivity and understanding, she argues, such books stupefy and harden the reader (148).

Like the arguments of Praz and Todorov, Napier's arguments apply well to the Gothic texts written by men before 1865 but not to the texts written by women. Despite Praz's assertions, female Gothic is not a clone of male Gothic. If, as Leslie Fiedler and David Punter have argued, male Gothic thumbs its nose at established literary conventions and is, therefore, somewhat subversive, "female gothic took the form of the subversion of the subversive" (Restuccia 264).[4] Despite its neglect by academic critics, the female Gothic tradition is far from being a freakish sideshow in the history of literature. Rather, it has been a significant literary force from the eighteenth century to the present, influencing virtually all English novelists, from the most profound to the most formulaic. Indeed, all major (that is, presently canonical) women novelists in England from 1790 to 1865 wrote at least some of their fiction in the Gothic mode. The fears that their texts explored resonated within many readers; Ann Radcliffe's novels made her "the most popular and best-paid English novelist of the eighteenth-century" (Moers 139), and Gothic novels in general have sold well for two hundred years.

In the 1790s, two significantly different types of Gothic literature
emerged in England, one written primarily by men and the other
written primarily by women. As critics like Praz and Todorov have
observed, male Gothic novelists from the 1790s to the 1860s lingered
over horrible spectacles of sexual violence, gore, and death, locating
evil in the "other"—women, Catholics, Jews, and ultimately the devil.
In contrast, female Gothic novelists uncovered the terror of the familiar: the routine brutality and injustice of the patriarchal family, conventional religion, and classist social structures.

Over the past two centuries, literary critics have fashioned many
accounts of differences between men's and women's writing. Arguing against the countless men who have discounted women's words
for millennia, some feminists have celebrated the special nature of
women's writing. Nineteenth- and early twentieth-century "romantic
feminists" believed that women were purer than men and that evidence of this purity often could be seen in women's writing (Jaggar 5).
More recently, French feminists like Luce Irigaray and Hélène Cixous
have imagined a feminine language (*écriture féminine*) that celebrates
woman's body, woman's sexual pleasure. In contrast to these feminists,
whose speculations about differences between men's and women's writing echo, at one level or another, the essentialism of patriarchal formulations of gender, I argue that the differences between male and
female Gothic texts written in England between 1790 and 1865 are
the result of two factors: differing political realities in the lives of the
male and female authors and the peculiar animosities that inspired
English novelists in the late eighteenth and early nineteenth centuries.

To be specific, substantial differences between male and female
Gothic traditions developed historically for the following reason:
Gothic fiction is primarily about fear, and the different subject positions that women and men have occupied in the world have produced
different experiences of fear.[5] In general, male writers of Gothic fiction appear to fear the suppressed power of the "other" (particularly
women) and therefore to delight in graphic descriptions of torture,
mutilation, and murder of women. Male Gothic plots before the mid-
nineteenth century often work to maintain the status quo by ensuring
the "legitimate" inheritance of property by the "appropriate" male
heir. The authors repeatedly thwart attempts by outsiders to take over
ancient family estates, and the texts depict brutal punishments of "de-
viant" women. In contrast, female writers of Gothic fiction fear the
unchecked power of men and therefore explore possibilities of resis-

tance to the patriarchal order. Female Gothic plots usually center on women trying to escape from decaying family estates and perverse patriarchs—perverse not because they deviate from normative social roles but because they fill their roles so exactly that their behavior calls attention to the injustice embedded in patriarchal ideology.

It should be noted that the different subject positions of men and women did not lead inevitably to misogyny on the one hand and feminism on the other. Charles Brockden Brown's 1798 American Gothic novel, *Wieland*, can easily be read as a feminist work; Clara Wieland, the narrator, is courageous, intelligent, and strong. The bizarre religious fanaticism of Clara's father and brother is represented as the main source of violence and suffering in the novel. Writing in the United States, Brown was more concerned with the peculiar religious and psychological dynamics of American life than with the sexual/textual battles taking place within British novels and between British novelists.[6]

Since Ellen Moers's ground-breaking essay "Female Gothic" was published in 1977, feminist criticism of the female Gothic tradition has been primarily psychoanalytic. Nathaniel Hawthorne anticipated that criticism of Gothic fiction (or "Romance") would focus on psychology; in *The House of the Seven Gables* (1851) he predicted that "modern psychology, it may be, will endeavor to reduce these alleged necromancies within a system, instead of rejecting them as altogether fabulous" (26). Ellen Moers fulfills Hawthorne's prediction by reading Mary Shelley's *Frankenstein* as a woman's birth myth that depicts "the trauma of afterbirth" (142). Sandra Gilbert and Susan Gubar extend Moers's analysis by arguing in *The Madwoman in the Attic* (1979) that Shelley's novel is a myth of origins told from Eve's perspective; as such, it is a comprehensive attack on the dominant philosophical ideas of her day.

Despite the interest in nineteenth-century women's writing stimulated by the work of critics like Moers and Gilbert and Gubar, few feminists have undertaken comprehensive reexaminations of the Gothic genre. In 1989 Kate Ferguson Ellis published the first book-length feminist study of the genre to focus on novels written by women: *The Contested Castle: Gothic Novels and the Subversion of Domestic Ideology.* Ellis insightfully argues that the Gothic "undermines and subverts" the eighteenth- and nineteenth-century idealization of the home as woman's place and man's haven (xvi). However, she ignores those aspects of Gothic texts that Praz, Todorov, and Napier identify as central to masculine Gothic; overlooking the differences between novels written by men and women leads her to ignore central features of the sexual/textual power struggle inscribed in Gothic fiction from 1790 to 1865.

In 1990 Eugenia C. DeLamotte published the second book-length feminist study of the Gothic genre: *Perils of the Night: A Feminist Study of Nineteenth-Century Gothic*. Analyzing English and American texts written by both men and women, DeLamotte shows that although twentieth-century male critics have marginalized female Gothic, "women were (and are) the primary readers, protagonists, and creators of the genre" (9). Furthermore, "Radcliffe must be regarded as the center of the Gothic tradition, if only for the central place she held in the minds of critics and writers alike during the flood tide of Gothic romance" (10). DeLamotte's rich, provocative study argues that "Gothic terror has its primary source in an anxiety about boundaries," particularly "the boundaries of the self" (13–14). Because patriarchal society simultaneously isolates and violates women, anxieties about boundaries have "a special relevance to the psychology and social condition of women" (23). DeLamotte's work undoubtedly will encourage future critics to recenter their readings of the Gothic.

There were significant political differences between female Gothic novelists like Mary Wollstonecraft, Ann Radcliffe, Mary Shelley, Charlotte Brontë, and Emily Brontë, but they all were alarmed by the death-fixated, misogynist creations of male Gothic novelists, who often attacked female writers explicitly as well as implicitly. Horace Walpole, for example, called Wollstonecraft a "hyena in petticoats," an insult not only to Wollstonecraft but also to her daughter, Mary Shelley, who revered her mother's memory (Sunstein 306). William Beckford, the author of *Vathek* (1786), contemptuously dismissed women writers as "super-literary ladies" who should cross-stitch rather than write "interminable scribbleations" (qtd. in Kiely 43). Reacting against the emerging male tradition, female Gothic novelists exposed the terrors of patriarchy from the victims' points of view. In turn, male Gothic novelists reacted against the emerging female tradition by reinscribing violence against women in their texts. From the 1790s until the mid-nineteenth century, the Gothic genre was produced by a dynamic process of action, reaction, and counterreaction, a perpetual writing and rewriting. Juxtaposing *The Monk* by M. G. Lewis and *The Italian* by Ann Radcliffe illuminates some of the fundamental differences between male and female Gothic traditions as they developed in the 1790s.[7]

M. G. Lewis was heavily influenced by Ann Radcliffe's *The Mysteries of Udolpho* (1794) while writing *The Monk* (1796). According to C. F. McIntyre, Lewis told his mother that reading *The Mysteries of Udolpho* "gave him the inspiration" to finish *The Monk* (64). In turn, textual evidence shows that Radcliffe was responding to *The Monk* when she wrote *The Italian* (1797).[8] Thus the three novels "are interconnected in a complex web of influence, disagreement, and rejection" (Punter 62). Both *The Monk* and *The Italian* are set in exotic, Catholic, southern Europe, and both texts represent the exploits of a corrupt monk who is guilty of heinous crimes, including murder and incestuous rape. Ambrosio in *The Monk* kills his mother and rapes and murders his sister. Schedoni in *The Italian* has similar violent intentions: he murders his brother; abducts, forces into marriage, and stabs his sister-in-law; and attempts to murder his daughter while she is sleeping alone at midnight (a situation clearly filled with sexual threat). Lewis gives free rein to Ambrosio's desire to commit violence against women; indeed, he provides Ambrosio with supernatural help to fulfill his fantasies. In contrast, Radcliffe repeatedly circumvents Schedoni's violent endeavors. The striking similarities and subtle divergences in plot, theme, and characterization in these two novels reveal the extent to which Lewis and Radcliffe were deliberately writing in light of and against each other's work.

Lewis wrote *The Monk* very quickly at the age of twenty, without bothering to revise the many careless narrative inconsistencies. He consciously delighted in complicating the plot and using multiple narrative frames, but the book's perverse antieroticism appears unselfconscious, which leads the reader to suspect that it expresses Lewis's own views towards women and sexuality.[9] *The Monk* opens in a church where the hero (Lorenzo) first sees the heroine (Antonia) and her aunt. The narrator's misogyny is immediately apparent in his description of the aunt, who is an "obstinate" old woman with shocking red hair, squinting eyes, and no sense of decorum. Her most ridiculous trait, as Lewis presents it, is that she likes to talk, in contrast to his heroine, a "lady" who is painfully embarrassed by her aunt's behavior and appears almost incapable of speech. After much hesitation, she does speak, but "in a voice so low as to be scarcely intelligible" (38). Mocking the aunt and lingering lecherously over a detailed physical description of Antonia, the narrator establishes a tone of contempt for women that he will maintain throughout the novel.

Reacting to Lewis, Radcliffe opens the first chapter of *The Italian* with a sentence that emphasizes the parallel structure of the two

novels: "It was in the church of San Lorenzo at Naples . . . that Vin-
centio di Vivaldi [the hero] first saw Ellena Rosalba [the heroine]" with
Signora Bianchi (her aunt) (5). Radcliffe proceeds, however, to depict
women in a respectful manner. Ellena's aunt is a dignified, though
frail, older woman who loves and protects Ellena to the best of her
ability. Describing the relationship between these women enables Radcliffe to begin her analysis of the economic injustice to which women
are subjected. Lacking a family fortune, Ellena must work diligently
to provide for her aunt and herself. She sews beautiful clothes but,
because she is unwilling to face society's contempt towards working
women, she must sell her work secretly and at a substantial disad-
vantage. Forced to "cautiously conceal" from the world "a knowledge
of the industry, which did honor to her character," she is nonetheless "the sole support of her aunt's declining years" (9). Lewis depicts
women as natural rivals and enemies; Radcliffe depicts them as allies
against an unjust social order. She also shows how the economic interests of socially advantaged women like the Marchesa di Vivaldi and the
Abbess of San Stefano pervert their moral understanding and cause
them to harm other women.

Ambrosio, Lewis's protagonist, is a saintly monk who is tempted into
depravity by Matilda, a demon disguised as a woman. Having fallen
from chastity into sex, Ambrosio finds that he cannot control his physical appetites. He savagely beats and strangles his mother when she
interrupts his attempts to rape his sister. The narrator describes Ambrosio gazing at his mother's corpse in the following manner: "Ambrosio beheld before him that once noble and majestic form, now become
a corpse, cold, senseless, and disgusting" (297). The verb "become"
removes Ambrosio's agency from the murder—Ambrosio is a voyeur
rather than a murderer. The mother's body has "become" a corpse;
it is this corpse, rather than Ambrosio's violent action, that the narrator describes as "disgusting." The sentence naturalizes Ambrosio's
actions, in keeping with the primary function of ideological language,
which is to obscure human responsibility (Barthes 151).

Later in *The Monk*, when a mob attacks the prioress of a convent, the
fury of the narration matches the fury of the mob:

> Wild with terror . . . the woman shrieked for a moment's mercy. . . .
> They refused to listen to her: they shewed her every sort of insult,
> loaded her with mud and filth, and called her by the most opprobrious
> appellations. They tore her from one another, and each new tormentor

was more savage than the former. They stifled with howls and execrations her shrill cries for mercy, and dragged her through the streets, spurning her, trampling her, and treating her with every species of cruelty which hate or vindictive fury could invent. At length a flint, aimed by some well-directing hand, struck her full upon the temple. She sank upon the ground, and in a few minutes terminated her miserable existence. Yet though she no longer felt their insults, the rioters still exercised their impotent rage upon her lifeless body. They beat it, trod upon it, and ill-used it, till it became no more than a mass of flesh, unsightly, shapeless, and disgusting. (344)

Once again, Lewis transforms a powerful female character into a "disgusting" corpse. As Todorov observes, in (male) fantasy, "the transformation of an attractive woman into a corpse is the pattern, repeated time and again" (136). Lewis takes this deadly transformation further than most male Gothic writers; the mob mutilates the female body until it is rendered shapeless and unrecognizable—"a mass of flesh."

After drugging his sister Antonia, Ambrosio incarcerates her in a tomb. The narrator describes the scene in necrophilic terms: "By the side of three putrid half-corrupted bodies lay the sleeping beauty" (363). Ambrosio whispers to her, "For your sake, fatal beauty! . . . for your sake have I committed this murder, and sold myself to eternal tortures" (364). Blaming her for his lust, he rapes her "with the rudeness of an unprincipled barbarian . . . and, in the violence of his lustful delirium, wounded and bruised her tender limbs" (368). Using words like "delirium" and "tender limbs," Lewis attempts to eroticize the violence of the rape. Fittingly, Ambrosio states, "This sepulchre seems to me Love's bower," underscoring his equation of love with death, an equation well established in the dominant literary discourse (366).

Lewis confuses even maternal love with necrophilia, as a scene with Agnes, a secondary character in the novel, illustrates. Entombed alive and slowly starving, Agnes gives birth to a baby who dies quickly but painfully. Describing her ordeals after a miraculous rescue, Agnes says, "I covered [the baby's corpse] with kisses, talked to it, wept, and moaned over it without remission day or night. . . . It soon became a mass of putridity, and to every eye was a loathsome and disgusting object, to every eye but a mother's. . . . I persisted in holding my infant to my bosom, in lamenting it, loving it, adoring it! . . . I endeavored to retrace its features through the livid corruption with which they were overspread. During my confinement, this sad occupation was my only delight" (393). Later, she says, "My slumbers were constantly interrupted by some obnoxious insect crawling over me. Sometimes I felt the bloated toad, hideous and pampered with the poisonous vapours of the dungeon, dragging his loathsome length along my bosom. Sometimes the cold lizard roused me, leaving his slimy track upon my face, and entangling itself in the tresses of my wild and matted hair. Often have I at waking found my fingers ringed with the long worms which bred in the corrupted flesh of my infant" (395–96). Lewis's repugnance towards sexuality is revealed in the plethora of slimy phallic images mingled with putrefaction in this passage.

Women who are at all self-assertive in *The Monk* are tortured or killed. Ambrosio's mother interrupts his attempts to rape Antonia; therefore, he kills her. The prioress has abused her power in the convent; therefore, the mob murders her. Agnes has been sexually indiscreet; therefore, the nuns entomb her alive. Like millions of people before and after him, Lewis suggests that the victim is to blame for her own suffering.

In any society where there is an unequal distribution of wealth and power, blaming victims for their own suffering serves the interests of the dominant group. Alice Miller suggests that the tendency to blame victims is rooted in childhood, when parents, the dominant force in the family, teach small children that "all the cruelty shown [them] in [their] upbringing is a punishment for [their] wrongdoing." As a result, "for many people it is very difficult to accept the sad truth that cruelty is often inflicted upon the innocent" (*For Your Own Good* 158). People who have been subjected to what Miller calls "poisonous pedagogy" are thus prepared to interpret suffering as a just punishment for the victims' immoral behavior. In a classist society, the poor are blamed for their poverty (they must be lazy, stupid, and incompetent or they wouldn't be poor). In a patriarchal society, women are blamed for everything from the fall of man onwards. M. G. Lewis reproduces this "poisonous pedagogy" by blaming women for the violence inflicted upon them by men.

Unlike Lewis, Radcliffe explicitly exposes the self-interested motives that lead dominant groups to blame victims for suffering. In *The Mysteries of Udolpho*, Montoni reacts to Emily's firm resistance of him with the twisted logic of poisonous pedagogy: "I must pity the weakness of mind, which leads you to so much suffering as you are compelling me to prepare for you" (381). Emily, who has learned to recognize Montoni's perverse reasoning for what it is, "with mild dignity" replies: "The strength of my mind is equal to the justice of my cause" (381).

In *The Italian*, Radcliffe continues her analysis of the linguistic strategies by which people gain and maintain power over others, showing how the dominant class will ultimately assert that violators of the social code deserve death.

The villains in *The Italian*, Father Schedoni (also called the Confessor) and the Marchesa di Vivaldi, conspire to advance their economic interests. Combining the power and resources of religion with the power and resources of the aristocracy, they pursue their plans with little fear of reprisal. The Marchesa's son, Vivaldi, falls in love with Ellena, an orphan with little money and apparently no important family connections. When Ellena accepts and returns Vivaldi's love, the Confessor and the Marchesa are enraged by the prospect of a lower-class woman marrying into the powerful Vivaldi family. The Marchesa exclaims, " 'The woman who obtrudes herself upon a family, to dishonour it . . . deserves a punishment nearly equal to that of a state criminal, since she injures those who best support the state. She ought to suffer—' 'Not nearly, but quite equal,' interrupt[s] the Confessor, 'she deserves—death!' " (168). Justifying their insatiable desire for profit by arguing that inter-class love threatens the state as much as treason, the Confessor and the Marchesa ultimately conclude that they have the right, indeed the moral obligation, to execute their enemies. Through exposing their logic, Radcliffe shows how love that crosses class lines threatens the ruling class. Her analysis anticipates the arguments of Freud and psychoanalytic feminists that "sexuality, which supposedly unites the couple, disrupts the kingdom if uncontrolled; it, too, must be contained and organized" in order for the patriarchal order to reproduce itself (Mitchell 405).

In the beginning of *The Monk*, Lewis's narrator suggests that the unnatural rigor of Catholicism, especially the sexual abstinence imposed upon priests, is responsible for Ambrosio's fall. Ultimately, however, the narrative locates the source of evil in the supernatural. Ambrosio is tempted into sin by a supernatural agent (whom he sees as a woman), and his most horrific crime, from the narrator's point of view, is selling his soul to the devil (who works through sex). By the late eighteenth century, this traditional Faustian sin was already a narrative cliché—a predictable moral pretext for a novel that indulged in pornographic fantasy.

In contrast to Lewis, Radcliffe locates the source of evil in human beings. She repeatedly expresses in *The Italian* a sense of anger and bewilderment at the human capacity for evil, especially the human ability to manipulate language to disguise self-interest and moral monstrosity. Rather than lingering over the horrible details of human suffering, Radcliffe emphasizes the terror of living in a world where man-made evil is always threatening and often realized. When she describes (anachronistically) the horrors of the Inquisition in *The Italian*, she does not make us witness actual scenes of torture; instead, she describes how hearing the moans of tortured prisoners and seeing the Inquisitors' gruesome instruments of death affect the hero psychologically.

Witnessing injustice fosters rebellion in Radcliffe's heroines and heroes. Vivaldi, a privileged son of the aristocracy, is shocked into a radical understanding of the world when he challenges social mores by falling in love with the "wrong" woman. He soon asks, "Is power then . . . the infallible test of justice?" (121). Thrown into the prisons of the Inquisition, he meditates on its horrors and

> los[es] every selfish consideration in astonishment and indignation of the sufferings, which the frenzied wickedness of man prepared for man, who, even at the moment of infliction, insults his victim with assertions of the justice and necessity of such procedure. "Is this possible!" said Vivaldi internally, "Can this be in human nature!—Can such horrible perversion of right be permitted! Can man, who calls himself endowed with reason, and immeasurably superior to every other created being, argue himself into the commission of such horrible folly, such inveterate cruelty, as exceeds all the acts of the most irrational and ferocious brute. Brutes do not deliberately slaughter their own species; it remains for man only, man, proud of his prerogative of reason, and boasting of his sense of justice, to unite the most terrible extremes of folly and wickedness!" (198)

Radcliffe's Gothic novels, like other Gothic novels by women, often express "astonishment and indignation" at the violence of patriarchal society. While M. G. Lewis adopted the role of Gothic "terrorist" to work as an agent of the state inscribing the dominant ideology (he was in fact a member of Parliament, a diplomatic attaché [spy] in The Hague, and an absentee slave-owner), Ann Radcliffe turned "terrorist" in implicit recognition of her position as a disenfranchised alien who could sabotage the dominant ideology.

Ultimately, however, Radcliffe withdrew from the linguistic battlefield. She carefully protected her privacy during her lifetime, and her husband apparently destroyed her personal papers after her death; therefore, little information about Radcliffe has survived outside her

novels, poetry, and travel book.[10] However, it is likely that, as a member
of the middle class, Radcliffe was alarmed or depressed by the gloomy
analysis of society that developed as she wrote *The Italian*. She also
may have been unable to recover from her distress over the unconscio-
nable productions of imitators who professed admiration of her work
but attempted to titillate audiences with graphic depictions of violence
against women. In particular, she must have been shocked by the "ultimate degradation of the Gothic sentimental heroine that the Marquis
de Sade cynically delineated in his *Justine*" (Murray 19). In any case,
after *The Italian* was published, Radcliffe lapsed into silence. She was
thirty-three years old, and she had "experienced a popularity which no
novelist before her—not Henry Fielding, not Samuel Richardson, not
Tobias Smollett, not Laurence Sterne—had come close to achieving"
(Murray 19). Despite a public eager for her work, she did not publish
another novel during the remaining twenty-six years of her life.

Gothic novels written by men between 1790 and 1865 often express
a rage that is part of the son's Oedipal rebellion against the father's
law and power.[11] At the same time, these texts usually claim male su-
premacy as a natural right and celebrate the ways in which the powerful impose their will over others. In contrast, female Gothic novels
express the pain and anger of permanently alienated daughters. Sons
may kill the father in order to take his place, but the only hope for
daughters is to overthrow the entire patriarchal system.

CLAIMING A VOICE AS AN AFRICAN AMERICAN WOMAN

In *Incidents in the Life of a Slave Girl*, Harriet Jacobs often meditates on
the pain of being silenced and celebrates moments of self-expression
as triumphs against her oppressors. Near the end of her narrative, she
observes, "Hot weather brings out snakes and slaveholders, and I like
one class of the venomous creatures as little as I do the other. What a
comfort it is, to be free to *say* so!" (174). By connecting freedom to verbal expression, Jacobs placed herself in a long tradition of oppressed
people struggling to write/right their own stories.

Ever since women first put pen to paper, they have described the
difficulties of gaining a voice in a patriarchal society. Although the
production of artistic work has been painful for many men, women
have struggled against many social demands and constrictions that

men have never had to face. In the words of Anne Finch, Countess of Winchilsea (1661–1720):

> Alas! A woman that attempts the pen
> Such an intruder on the rights of men,
> Such a presumptuous Creature is esteem'd
> The fault can by no vertue be redeem'd.[12]

Classic works of feminist literary criticism, including Virginia Woolf's *A Room of One's Own*, Tillie Olsen's *Silences*, and Sandra Gilbert and Susan Gubar's *The Madwoman in the Attic*, have described the social pressures that often silence women. Since the late 1960s, countless feminist critics have documented and analyzed the exclusion of female authors from the academic canon.[13]

By this time, then, it should be clear that all women writers confront social and psychological constrictions against their writing that are specifically based on gender. However, many additional constrictions are based on race and class. The ongoing popularity and commercial success of women's Gothic novels compared to the quick disappearance of women's slave narratives after the American Civil War dramatizes this fact. Juxtaposing the experiences of white and black women writers forces us to reexamine the complexities of power relations in a patriarchal society that is also racist and classist. In relation to white men, white women were substantially disadvantaged in the nineteenth-century literary and political world. However, in relation to black women, white women wielded substantial power, which they used and abused in a variety of ways.

Since the eighteenth century, novels have been produced and consumed mainly by women. Because the novel has always attracted a broad popular audience, many novelists have not been dependent on the academy or on established (white male) critics for financial success. Thus, although female Gothic novels have been neglected and abused by critics, they have always maintained a wide readership. Ann Radcliffe was a best-selling author whose influence was widely acknowledged by nineteenth-century writers.[14] Jane Austen was beloved by readers in her own day and is considered by many twentieth-century critics (even nonfeminists like F. R. Leavis and Ian Watt) to be one of the greatest novelists in the English language. Mary Shelley's monster quickly became and has remained a central figure in popular mythology, and Charlotte Brontë's *Jane Eyre* and Emily Brontë's *Wuthering Heights* have been purchased by millions of readers for over 150 years. Insofar as a canon of women's literature has emerged in Anglo-American feminist circles since the 1960s, all the novelists mentioned above (with the ironic exception of Ann Radcliffe) have secured a central place.

Women's slave narratives have suffered a fate quite different from that of women's Gothic novels. To begin with, nineteenth-century African Americans of both genders had extremely restricted access to education; most were denied even basic literacy. Those who did manage to write had access to significantly different and more limited modes of publication than British novelists. To compound their difficulties in claiming a voice, African American women encountered social definitions of womanhood that diminished white women but excluded black women altogether. And finally, although white women's writing has been marginalized in the academy, a perverse mixture of racism and sexism has made nineteenth-century black women's writing virtually invisible.

White women in Britain between 1790 and 1865 were excluded from institutions of higher education, and this exclusion was a painful deprivation to women who were eager for intellectual stimulation and discipline. During the same period, however, most black American slaves were forbidden to learn even the basic skills of reading and writing. Slaveholders used every linguistic resource they could imagine to make their power appear absolute and unassailable. They constructed religious, biological, and legal justifications for their domination of women and slaves, arguing that the power of the white paterfamilias was ordained by God, made evident in nature, and sanctioned by law. Any black person who took mastery of the English language challenged the entire ideological construct of American slavery—and he or she risked severe punishment. Slaves understood that power is "negotiated through speech acts," and they constantly waged a linguistic war against their masters, often talking their "way out of the most abject forms of humiliation" (Andrews, *To Tell* 278). However, slaveholders often used savage force to silence the people they enslaved. In addition to beating, starving, and murdering slaves, masters sometimes placed a "bit" (an iron tongue) in slaves' mouths to enforce silence, a device that inflicted acute physical and psychological pain.[15]

While speech was dangerous for slaves, reading and writing were absolutely forbidden in many states. Laws against teaching slaves literacy underscore slaveholders' recognition of the importance of their control of language. Antiliteracy laws were enacted as early as 1740, when a South Carolina statute declared:

> *whereas* the having of slaves taught to write, or suffering them to be employed in writing, may be attended with great inconveniences; *Be it enacted,* that all and every person and persons whatsoever, who shall hereafter teach, or cause any slave or slaves to be taught to write, or shall use or employ any slave as a scribe in any manner of writing whatsoever, hereafter taught to write; every such person or persons shall, for every offense, forfeith the sum of one hundred pounds current money. (qtd. in Gates, "Writing 'Race'" 9)

Restrictions against literacy grew more severe in the nineteenth century, as slaveholders became increasingly fearful of slave revolts. In fact, "in some places it became a crime merely to sell writing materials to slaves" (Genovese 562). Yet slaveholders could not kill the slaves' desire to learn; "literate slaves appeared everywhere, no matter how unfavorable the atmosphere" (Genovese 563). Slave narratives, by their mere existence, demonstrated that slaveholders' power was *not* absolute and that black people were intelligent human beings. Thus the texts were always, inevitably, subversive.[16]

The authors of slave narratives were well aware of the subversive nature of their writing; Frederick Douglass, for example, observed that "there are special reasons why I should write my own biography. . . . Not only is slavery on trial, but unfortunately, the enslaved people are also on trial. It is alleged, that they are, naturally, inferior; that they are so low in the scale of humanity, and so utterly stupid, that they are unconscious of their wrongs, and do not apprehend their rights" (*My Bondage* 4). In his writing and his speaking, Douglass powerfully demonstrated the full humanity of enslaved people.

Significantly, it was often courageous, compassionate white women and children who clandestinely taught slaves to read and write. In turn many slaves, at the risk of their lives, taught other slaves. Both Frederick Douglass and Harriet Jacobs were taught the beginnings of literacy by kindly mistresses, and they derived intense pleasure from passing on their knowledge to their fellow slaves. White women sometimes felt it was their Christian duty to teach slaves to read the Bible; a few mistresses expressed tentative feelings of sympathy and kinship with the oppressed slaves. Catherine Devereaux Edmondston wrote in 1860 that she and many other slave-holding women felt guilty for *not* teaching their slaves: "This teaching of Negroes is a sore problem to me! It ought to be done and I ought to do it. . . . My difficulties I am convinced beset many a well-intentioned mistress who, like me, does nothing because she cannot do what she feels she *ought*" (qtd. in Genovese 564). While Edmondston was distressed by the legal restrictions against teaching slaves, some mistresses "scoffed at the law" and taught slaves despite the risks (Genovese 563).

Those exceptional American slaves who managed to acquire literacy and to escape from slavery still faced tremendous obstacles against representing their experiences and ideas in their own words. White northerners were usually no more receptive to the stories of African Americans than white southerners, and without support from whites, African Americans had little access to publication. Aware of this problem, many African Americans in the North attempted to establish independent publishing institutions. In fact, "by 1830 more than fifty black anti-slavery societies had been founded, and several anti-slavery publications had been initiated. . . . In 1827 the first black newspaper, *Freedman's Journal*, began publication in New York City" (Furman 123). However, these societies and publishers lacked the resources to promote widespread African American literary activity. The sad fate of Harriet E. Wilson and her autobiographical novel, *Our Nig* (1859), is representative of the general fate of nineteenth-century African American writers and their texts.

Our Nig was the first novel written by an African American to be published in the United States. In many ways, it is "an allegory of a slave narrative, a 'slave' narrative set in the 'free' North" (Carby 43). In it, Wilson compellingly describes northern racism, "showing that slavery's shadows fall even there" (subtitle). Apparently because of its attack on northern hypocrisy and its sympathetic portrayal of a marriage between a white woman and a black man (the parents of the heroine), the novel did not appeal to any influential white readers. Determined to get her story into print despite the lack of white patronage, Wilson published it at her own expense, addressing it to her "colored brethren" who she hoped would "rally around me a faithful band of supporters and defenders" (Preface). George C. Rand and Avery of Boston printed at least one hundred copies at the author's expense, but the novel attracted little attention. In fact, not a single review of it was ever published, despite the fact that Boston was at the time "a veritable center of abolitionist reform and passion, and [there was] a growing black press eager to celebrate all black achievement in the arts and sciences" (Gates xxx). In his introduction to the novel's second edition (which was published in 1983, 124 years after the first edition), Henry Louis Gates laments the virtual disappearance of Harriet E. Wilson from history, observing that, after painstaking efforts, "we have been able to account for her existence only from 1850 to 1860" (xiv).

The history of African American literature in the eighteenth and nineteenth centuries indicates that only those texts that, for one reason or another, attracted a white audience had a chance of surviving in the white-dominated world of literature. Phillis Wheatley, the first African American to author a book, attracted attention partly because she was seen by whites as an anomaly, a curiosity. Gates points out that Wheatley was examined by "eighteen of Boston's most notable citizens" who set themselves up as a jury to determine whether or not she, a black woman, was actually capable of writing poetry. The "attestation" of these judges was necessary in order for Wheatley to publish her *Poems on Various Subjects, Religious and Moral* in 1773 (Gates, "Foreword" viii–ix). Apparently, one black poet was enough to satisfy white curiosity—until 1829 Wheatley remained "the *only* black person to have published a book of imaginative literature in English" ("Foreword" x).

The slave narrative genre exists not only because of the remarkable efforts of black authors but also because it was a form of writing supported by a powerful group of white political reformers. John Sekora has shown that the genre has roots in narratives written as early as 1703, and "by the early 1830s at the latest, sponsors, printers, and reviewers were writing of a distinct literary genre. Certainly readers were by then normally calling accounts of slave life, as related by a present or former slave, 'slave narratives'" ("Black Message" 484). Slaves' stories continued to be recorded at least until 1938, when the Federal Writers' Project of the Works Progress Administration finished gathering oral histories. However, because of its usefulness as antislavery propaganda, the slave narrative genre was fostered in a distinctive way between 1830 and 1865 by the abolitionist movement. Abolitionists supplied funds, regulations, and a purpose for the narratives, which were usually marketed for a wide, predominantly white audience. Between 1845 and 1849, the narratives written by Frederick Douglass, William Wells Brown, and James W. C. Pennington "far outsold anything published by Thoreau, Hawthorne, or Melville during the same years" (MacKethan 55). However, all three ex-slave writers were employed by the Boston Anti-Slavery Society, and their writings were considered political propaganda, not art. White abolitionists did not expect slave narratives to be read after the immediate political goal—the abolition of slavery—was achieved.

As William L. Andrews shows in *To Tell a Free Story*, white abolitionists were often insidiously racist. This racism was evident in the many restrictions they placed on black autobiographers. White abolitionists wanted ex-slaves to describe the "hard facts" of slavery, not to explore the development of their perceptions of self and society. Ex-slaves who wanted to tell their stories could observe that, in the white supremacist American culture, "by implication the truth of a slave narrative is proportionate to the degree of objectification achieved by the narrator. The more distance he can place between himself as perceiving ego and as receiving, transmitting eye, the more his story will be assumed to approach reality" (Andrews, *To Tell* 63). Many African Americans resented the ways white abolitionists objectified and used ex-slaves and their texts. Anthony G. Barthelemy points out that some African Americans told their life stories to abolitionists only out of financial desperation. For example, Louisa Picquet, a former slave and "concubine," answered the "prying and often lewd questions" of the Reverend Hiram Mattison, who wrote her narrative in 1861, because "she needed money to rescue her mother from whom she had been separated for nearly twenty years" (xl). Barthelemy persuasively argues that "Picquet clearly understands her relationship to Mattison. Once again, she is on the block; something is for sale" (xli). Like many white readers, Mattison was obsessed with the details of black women's sexual experiences and with the shocking but seductive specter of miscegenation.[17]

Like Louisa Picquet's veiled and sometimes ironic responses to Mattison's questions, the final chapter of Harriet Wilson's novel also expresses resentment against abolitionists' self-serving use of black voices. With a mixture of moral censure and amused sympathy, Wilson's narrator describes an attractive black man, Samuel, who pretends to be an escaped slave and is hired by abolitionists to go on lecturing tours. He marries the novel's heroine, Frado, but soon abandons her, "with the disclosure that he had never seen the South, and that his illiterate harangues were humbugs for hungry abolitionists" (128). Wilson's subtle irony is wonderfully evident in this sentence: the word "illiterate" is followed by the alliteration and consonance of "harangues," "humbugs," and "hungry," which suggest that although

Samuel might be formally unschooled, he certainly is not unskilled with language. The narrator, who repeatedly draws analogies between southern and northern racism, concludes the novel by comparing abolitionists to the dreaded kidnappers who terrorized ex-slaves and free blacks. Frado finds herself "watched by kidnappers [and] maltreated by abolitionists, who didn't want slaves at the South, nor niggers in their own houses, North" (129).

White audiences did not expect humor, irony, or linguistic subtleties in the texts of ex-slaves. Rather, they wanted to read slave narratives as passive reflections of the "facts" of slavery. The anonymous editor of Douglass's second autobiography expresses a prevalent abolitionist view when he describes Douglass's text in the following terms: "If the volume now presented to the public were a mere work of ART, the history of its misfortune might be written in two very simple words— TOO LATE. The nature and character of slavery have been subjects of an almost endless variety of artistic representation. . . . The reader is, therefore, assured, with all due promptitude, that his attention is not invited to a work of ART, but to a work of FACTS—Facts, terrible and almost incredible, it may be—yet FACTS, nevertheless" (*My Bondage* 3). Although this editor implies that art is artful and inferior to history, he also asserts that only writers who "possess the charm of transcendent exellence [*sic*]" should attempt to achieve art. He assures readers that Douglass knows his place; he will stick to "the facts of his remarkable history" (5).

The white reader's expectation that a reliable slave narrator would be a selfless, objective "transmitting eye," rather than a complex, intelligent interpreter of the world contrasts sharply with readers' expectations for Gothic novels. Female Gothic was marked by and loved for its focus on the heroine's sensibility and, increasingly, on her psychological development. Indeed, Raymond Williams argues that Charlotte Brontë "stands very obviously at the head of a tradition. . . . I mean that fiction in which the only major emotion, and then the relation with the reader, is that exact stress, that first-person stress: 'circumstanced like me'" (73–74). Williams is wary of and exhausted by "this shaping longing demanding consciousness" (74), but the popularity of *Jane Eyre* from the time it was published in 1847 to the present suggests that many readers relish Brontë's exploration of Jane's consciousness. Many readers, like Adrienne Rich, have even found in *Jane Eyre* "some nourishment . . . a special force and survival value" ("Jane Eyre" 89).

Feminists have long been aware of the fact that Charlotte Brontë overcame many obstacles that could easily have prevented her from writing. She wrote despite severe financial strain, limited access to education, humiliating outside employment, and frequent emotional exhaustion induced by her father's and brother's constant demands. Like many nineteenth-century female novelists, she and her sisters adopted neuter pen names in hopes of gaining criticism of their writing that was not gender-based. Nonetheless, Brontë had an advantage as an author that no African American woman had. Because Brontë was a member of the British middle class, a large group of readers could recognize her writing as part of a significant tradition of literature. Men might sneer, but women would continue buying and reading female Gothic fiction.

Writing at the same time as Brontë, black women like Harriet Jacobs wrote against restrictions that were on every point more severe than those Brontë encountered. While patriarchal ideology made it difficult for white women to write or to speak simply because they were women, racist ideology made it even more difficult for black women to write or to speak because they were *not* seen as women. They were seen as even less than women—subhuman and bestial. Thus, as Hazel Carby observes, "In order to gain a public voice as orators or published writers, black women had to confront the dominant domestic ideologies and literary conventions of womanhood that excluded them from the definition 'woman'" (6).

In 1851 Sojourner Truth electrified a hostile white audience at a women's rights convention in Akron, Ohio, by boldly indicting patriarchal power and conventional notions of womanhood:

> I think that 'twixt all the niggers of the South and the women at the North all a talking 'bout rights, the white men will be in a fix pretty soon. . . . That man over there say a woman needs to be helped into carriages and lifted over ditches, and to have the best place everywhere. Nobody ever helped me into carriages, or over mud puddles, or gives me any best place and ain't I a woman? Look at me! Look at my arm! I have plowed, and planted, and gathered into barns, and no man could head me—and ain't I a woman? I could work as much and eat as much as a man (when I could get it), and bear the lash as well—and ain't I a woman? I have borne thirteen children and seen em mos' all sold off into slavery, and when I cried out with a mother's grief, none but Jesus heard me—and ain't I a woman? [18]

Truth's challenge—"Ain't I a Woman?"—resonates throughout the texts of nineteenth-century African American women. For them to claim a place as a woman meant claiming a place as a human being in opposition to the racist, patriarchal ideology that defined black women as chattel.[19]

In *Incidents in the Life of a Slave Girl*, Harriet Jacobs repeatedly emphasized that "no pen can give an adequate description of the all-pervading corruption produced by slavery" (51). This statement has multivalent meanings. First, Jacobs, like hundreds of writers before her, was pointing to the inadequacy of language to express the human pain and degradation that existed under slavery. Second, Jacobs was keenly aware of the difficulties of breaking silences, not only about racial oppression but also about enslaved women's particular oppression. She stated truthfully, "I have not exaggerated the wrongs inflicted by Slavery; on the contrary, my descriptions fall far short of the facts" (1). Nonetheless, she courageously and brilliantly overcame multiple social constrictions by writing her narrative, which is perhaps the longest and best-developed slave narrative ever written by a woman.

After Harriet Jacobs managed to write her story, she struggled for several years to get it published. The publication history of *Incidents in the Life of a Slave Girl* itself reveals the complex relationships of enmity and solidarity between white and black women. By emphasizing the particular ways in which *women* were oppressed by patriarchal slavery, Jacobs appealed to the feminist beliefs of many abolitionist women. She addressed her text to white northern women, hoping to "arouse" them "to a realizing sense of the condition of two millions of women at the South, still in bondage, suffering what I suffered, and most of them far worse" (1). Jean Fagan Yellin shows that Jacobs learned from her interactions with Harriet Beecher Stowe that white abolitionist women often could not be trusted (Introduction xviii–xix). However, Jacobs found in feminist-abolitionists such as Amy Post and Lydia Maria Child "the kind of implied reader who Jacobs needed to believe was out there in the white world ready to listen empathetically to her story" (Andrews, *To Tell* 247).

Like other nineteenth-century (ex-)slave writers, Jacobs not only needed to believe that a sympathetic readership existed for her text; she also needed references and editorial assistance from established white women writers. Amy Post encouraged Jacobs and introduced her to influential literary figures. Finally Lydia Maria Child was enlisted to "edit" the narrative. She rearranged several sections but, unlike many "editors" of slave narratives, she did not ghost-write or substantially change Jacobs's text. Child stated (accurately, according to

Yellin) that "I abridged, and struck out superfluous words sometimes; but I don't think I *altered* fifty words in the whole volume" (qtd. by Yellin xxii). Nonetheless, the scholars who read Jacobs's narrative after the Civil War doubted both Jacobs's authorship and the authenticity of the events she describes. Not until 1981, when Yellin painstakingly researched and documented the existence of Harriet Jacobs and the plausibility of the incidents Jacobs describes, did critics begin to treat the narrative in a serious manner.

For most white readers from the eighteenth century to the present, slave narratives lack credibility unless "authenticated" by members of the very class that oppressed their authors. This "authentication" has taken several forms. Before 1865, the narratives were usually enclosed by white-authored texts (letters, prefaces, bills of sale, and so on), and they were often dictated to white amanuenses, edited by white writers, or both. Ironically, twentieth-century critics often have taken the presence of white-authored texts as reason to doubt the validity or integrity of the black-authored texts. These modern critics demand that modern scholars (usually white) once again authenticate the texts.

It is certainly true that eighteenth- and nineteenth-century African Americans wrote under severe restrictions and that these restrictions sometimes compromised their work. We need, however, to be wary of the assumption that art is produced by exceptional individuals working in isolation. *All* texts need to be read in the light of the historical contexts in which they are produced, and most texts are produced in conjunction with outside readers and editors. All texts also inevitably reproduce to some extent the dominant ideology of the culture in which they are written. These facts do not diminish the significance of authors' efforts to strengthen or to subvert the existing power structure. No human being is an autonomous free subject; nonetheless, "whatever limits we face, our power—ability and agency—lies in choice. . . . Moral agency involves the ability to go on under oppression: to continue to make choices, to act within the oppressive structure of our society and challenge oppression, to create meaning through our living" (Hoagland 13). The exceptional African Americans who recorded their experiences in slave narratives were acting within the oppressive structure of their society, as all writers must. However, they did so to challenge oppression, to make themselves "the subjects of [their] own narrative, witnesses to and participants in [their] own experience, and, in no way coincidentally, in the experience of those with whom [they came] in contact" (Morrison, "Unspeakable" 9). Against all odds, the authors of slave narratives persistently demonstrated their humanity. Like Toni Morrison, they insisted that "we are not, in fact, 'other.' We are choices" (9).

Like most literary genres, then, slave narratives are both products of historical conditions and willed artistic achievements. They provide more first-hand knowledge of slavery from the perspective of the enslaved than any other known body of literature in history, and they should be valued for the ways in which they represent aspects of history that are not accessible through any other medium. However, they should not be judged simply on the basis of whether or not they contain "hard facts" about slavery. Like texts in all literary genres, slave narratives contain insights about society, language, and the self that are not merely matters of historical "accuracy."

Many critics have interpreted the similarities between women's slave narratives and "sentimental" fiction as yet another reason to discount both genres. For these critics, the story of a vulnerable heroine fighting against the sexual designs of a powerful man is to be accounted as merely a literary convention. However, given the frequent reality and the perpetual threat of sexual violence against all women in patriarchal cultures and particularly against black women in American culture, it is not surprising that white and black women's writing repeatedly addresses issues of sexual aggression. This is not *mere* convention (whatever that means) but rather a convention that is based upon actual experiences and anxieties.

In *Hard Facts: Setting and Form in the American Novel*, Philip Fisher argues that from the late eighteenth to the mid-nineteenth century the sentimental novel was "the most radical popular form available to middle-class culture" (91). The central function of the genre was to arouse readers' compassion. Moreover, Fisher contends, "the political content of sentimentality is democratic in that it experiments with the extension of full and complete humanity to classes of figures from whom it has been socially withheld. The typical objects of sentimental compassion are the prisoner, the madman, the child, the very old, the animal, and the slave. Each achieves, or rather earns, the right to human regard by means of the reality of their suffering" (99). Fisher reminds us that "in the 18th century it was common to visit asylums to be entertained by the antics of the mad" (99). Sentimental novels such as *Uncle Tom's Cabin* helped to transform social consciousness by attempting to represent "full human reality" for disempowered members of society (99).

Fisher suggests that the political power of sentimental fiction is limited to arousing empathy rather than inciting action, but its "revision of images" accomplished important cultural work (122). His argument illuminates the reasons why slave narratives were an effective tool in the abolitionist struggle. Far from being diminished by adopting some of the conventions of sentimental fiction, slave narratives were strengthened by their kinship with another socially transformative genre. At the same time, sentimental novels like *Uncle Tom's Cabin* gained some of their social effectiveness by employing literary strategies borrowed from the female Gothic and slave narrative traditions.

From a Bakhtinian perspective, William L. Andrews also shows that slave narratives were enriched rather than compromised as they developed "features of what M. M. Bakhtin has called the 'novelization' of narrative genres" (*To Tell* 271–72). Harriet Jacobs in particular gains a great deal of power and richness in her narrative by her use of multiple languages—what Bakhtin calls heteroglossia. Jacobs is able to negotiate the contradictory but intersecting demands of sentimental, abolitionist, feminist, and Christian ideologies by including their multiple languages in her text. Her creation of the narrator, Linda Brent, is not only a practical move to disguise her identity but also an artistic move that enables her to distance herself somewhat from the self she represents. As Bakhtin says:

> The author is not to be found in the language of the narrator . . . but rather, the author utilizes now one language, now another, in order to avoid giving [her]self up wholly to either of them. . . . All forms involving a narrator or a posited author signify to one degree or another by their presence the author's freedom from a unitary and singular language, a freedom connected with the relativity of literary and language systems; such forms open up the possibility of never having to define oneself in language, the possibility of translating one's own intentions from one linguistic system to another, of fusing "the language of truth" with "the language of the everyday," of saying "I am me" in someone else's language, and in my own language, "I am other." (314–15)

In addition, by including dialogues between oppositional characters, excerpts of sermons, and stanzas of slaves' songs in her text, Jacobs calls attention to competing ideologies and advances the struggle to populate language with her own intention and desire.

The animosities that divide Gothic novels written by English women from Gothic novels written by English men do not generally pertain to slave narratives written by women and men. Male and female slaves understood that they shared a common enemy: the white supremacist patriarchal system of slavery. Women's slave narratives distinctively place sexual oppression at the heart of "the all-pervading corruption produced by slavery" (Jacobs 51), but men's slave narratives never evidence the virulent misogyny that characterizes many male Gothic novels. In fact, men's narratives sometimes reveal a great deal of sensitivity to the special oppression of women. The *Narrative of William W. Brown* (1847), for example, expresses Brown's pervasive distress about the abuse inflicted on his mother, his sister, and other slave women. His interest in women's rights is confirmed during his escape to the North. Desperately hungry, he stops at a farmhouse to ask for food. The man inside insults him and tries to turn him away, but the woman invites him in. She tells her husband "two or three times to get out of the way, and let me in. But as he did not move, she pushed him on one side, bidding me walk in! I was never before so glad to see a woman push a man aside! Ever since that act, I have been in favor of 'woman's rights'!" (222). Brown notes that this woman not only gives him "as much food as I could eat" and "ten cents, all the money then at her disposal," she also sends him "to a friend, a few miles further on the road" (222). This rebellious wife was part of a network of women who were determined to help fugitive slaves. Witnessing the brutal oppression of enslaved women as well as that of some white wives and daughters led many enslaved men to support women's struggles for liberation. Observing the central role that women played in the abolitionist movement often strengthened that support.

The greatest male representative of the slave narrative genre, Frederick Douglass, was an active feminist. Although his views on women's rights were sometimes problematic, he was clearly outraged by the sexual abuse of women and often lectured on women's rights.[20] He also recognized that, as a man, he was not well situated to analyze women's peculiar oppression. In the third chapter of *My Bondage and My Freedom*, he expresses horror at the "glaring odiousness" of a system whereby men routinely rape women and then profit financially by enslaving their own blood (42). He observes that "a whole volume might be written on this single feature of slavery," but "it is not within the scope of the design of my simple story, to comment upon every phase of slavery not within my experience as a slave" (42, 43).

Harriet Jacobs wrote the "whole volume" that Douglass called for, and she eloquently showed that "slavery is terrible for men; but it is far more terrible for women. Superadded to the burden common to all, *they* have wrongs, and sufferings, and mortifications peculiarly their own" (77). Douglass was sympathetic to the particular sufferings of women, but nonetheless he saw becoming free as the same thing as becoming a man. At the turning point in his *Narrative*, he states succinctly: "You have seen how a man was made a slave; you shall see how a slave was made a man" (97). The battle that transforms his life is a physical, violent fight with Covey, a notoriously sadistic slavebreaker. In contrast, Jacobs imagines freedom as the time when she will be able to control her sexuality and provide a home for herself and her children. The war of her life cannot be represented in one climactic fight; she must struggle unceasingly to deny Flint access to her body and mind. The self-image that Douglass most often projects is that of a great individualist fighting alone; in contrast, Jacobs usually represents herself as a simultaneous insider-outsider in relation to various households: the Flints', her grandmother's, and Mrs. Bruce's. The space she occupies in her "loop-hole of retreat" when hiding in her grandmother's attic for seven years represents the liminal space she occupies throughout the book. She is both liberated and imprisoned in other women's households, successfully escaping from the patriarch, Dr. Flint, but unable to own her own space.

Comparing the experiences of Jacobs and Douglass after their escapes to the North reveals that the peculiar wrongs, sufferings, and mortifications of women did not end with slavery. Jacobs (1813–97) and Douglass (1818–95) were well matched in age and abilities, and they authored the most impressive texts in the American slave narrative tradition. They fled to the North around the same time (Jacobs in 1842, Douglass in 1838), and they became acquaintances who shared many friends and many interests. However, just as slavery forced Jacobs and Douglass to endure different forms of exploitation, the gender structure of the North provided them with very different opportunities. Jacobs was employed as a domestic worker by her white female friends, and she completed her manuscript in 1858 only because of her remarkable perseverance. After the book was finally published in 1861, Jacobs attained a "limited celebrity" among abolitionists (Yellin, Introduction xxv). In subsequent years, she worked hard "distributing clothing and supplies and organizing schools, nursing homes, and orphanages," but by "the twentieth century both Jacobs and her book were forgotten" (xxv).

Frederick Douglass, in contrast, was strongly encouraged by abolitionists to assume a prominent public position through speaking and writing. In 1841 he was invited to speak at an abolitionist meeting and then was hired as a full-time antislavery lecturer. His best-selling *Narrative* was published in 1845, and he was encouraged to revise and expand it repeatedly during the next half-century (*My Bondage and My Freedom* in 1855 and *Life and Times of Frederick Douglass* in 1881). Douglass received active support from multiple sources, white and black, male and female. Like Jacobs, Douglass encountered substantial racism in his white friends, but, unlike Jacobs, he was able to analyze publicly the problematics of white racism by discussing his life in the North in his second and third autobiographies. In addition to his illustrious career as a speaker and writer, Douglass was appointed to several government positions (from U. S. marshall for the District of Columbia in 1877 to minister-general and consul-general to the Republic of Haiti and chargé d'affaires for Santo Domingo in 1891).

Douglass was a courageous advocate of women's rights from the beginning to the end of his career. In 1848 he "was the only man to take a prominent part in the proceedings" of the women's rights convention in Seneca Falls, New York, and he died of a heart attack almost fifty years later "upon returning home after speaking at a woman's rights meeting" (Quarles xxv–xxvi). But despite his concern about the oppression of women, he benefitted substantially from male gender privilege. In contrast to Jacobs, who was never permitted free sexual or emotional expression and who constantly had to nurture others while remaining deprived herself, Douglass had access to the emotional resources of numerous women.

In 1838 Douglass married Anna Murray, a free black woman from Baltimore who followed him to the North and devoted her life to providing for the material and emotional well-being of Douglass and their children. He was often absent for months (sometimes years) at a time, lecturing internationally as "a leader of the antislavery movement and a public figure who was most attractive to women" (Sterling 135). In an 1855 introduction to Douglass's second autobiography, Dr. James McCune Smith, a prominent black physician and abolitionist, describes the response of Englishwomen to Douglass in typical Victorian terms: "With that prompt and truthful perception which has led their sisters in all ages of the world to gather at the feet and support the hands of reformers, the gentlewomen of England were foremost to encourage and strengthen [Douglass] to carve out for himself a path fitted to his powers and energies, in the life-battle against slavery and caste to which he was pledged" (15). Although Smith demeans women's role in the abolitionist movement by representing women as worshiping helpers of men, he accurately observes that Douglass was emotionally and intellectually nurtured by women who shared his feminist-abolitionist agenda.

In 1848 a white woman named Julia Griffiths came from England to help Douglass with his work, and she lived with the Douglasses for three years, "reading aloud to Frederick when he was tired or depressed, worrying about his health, [and] travelling with him when he lectured outside the city" (Sterling 135). Meanwhile, Anna Douglass prided herself in providing a clean, comfortable home for her husband. Their daughter Rosetta observed, "Father was mother's honored guest. He was from home so often that his home comings were events that she thought worthy of extra notice. Every thing was done to add to his comfort" (qtd. in Sterling 137).

Clearly "freedom" offered different things to Douglass than it offered to Jacobs. With women washing his clothes, cooking his food, and taking care of his children, Douglass was able to devote his tremendous energies "to promot[ing] the moral, social, religious, and intellectual elevation of the free colored people; never . . . refusing, while Heaven lends me ability, to use my voice, my pen, or my vote, to advocate the great and primary work of the universal and unconditional emancipation of my entire race" (*My Bondage* 248). In contrast, Jacobs was left wondering what "freedom" meant and lamenting the fact that she was still deprived of "a home of my own," separated from her children and in service to a white woman (201). Whereas Douglass's time was liberated by the work of his female friends, Jacobs felt bound by "love, duty, [and] gratitude . . . to serve her who pities my oppressed people" (201).

Harriet Jacobs's *Incidents* articulates one of the most comprehensive analyses of gender and racial oppressions in all of nineteenth-century American literature. Thus it would seem reasonable for critics interested in the slave narrative genre or in nineteenth-century American women's writing in general to place Jacobs's text at the center of their work. Unfortunately, women's slave narratives virtually disappeared from consciousness from 1865 until the 1980s, when a few African-Americanist and feminist scholars worked to get them reprinted. The critical establishment is only beginning to address these texts seriously. William L. Andrews observes that although men's slave narratives have been ignored and neglected, they "have never been mentioned and then dismissed with the suspicion and condescension that Jacobs's book has repeatedly received" (*To Tell* 267). As Joanne Braxton points out, this dismissal of women's slave narratives is part of a pervasive social dismissal of black women's lives: "Academic systems that do not value scholarship on black women, or reward it, have told us that we are not first, not central, not major, not authentic, suggesting that neither the lives of black women nor the study of our narratives and autobiographies has been legitimate" (18).

In sum, the dominant American culture has used multiple strategies to exclude black women writers from serious study. The formulators of slavery refused to teach black people to read or write and then told them they were intellectually incapable of literacy and forbade them to attempt it. Then, if a black woman actually did write something, critics brought out all the old weapons used to suppress women's writing: "She didn't write it. She wrote it, but she shouldn't have. She wrote it, but look what she wrote about. She wrote it, but 'she' isn't really an artist, and 'it' isn't really serious, of the right genre—i.e. really art. She wrote it, but she only wrote one of it. She wrote it, but it's only interesting/included in the canon for one, limited reason. She wrote it, but there are very few of her" (Russ 76). It is not surprising that the texts that African American women wrote between 1790 and 1865 were many fewer in number and much shorter than the Gothic novels written by British women. What is surprising is the fact that antebellum African American women managed to write their stories at all, given the obstacles they encountered. Our appreciation of the remarkable literary accomplishments of Jacobs and the other female authors of slave narratives is strengthened when we understand the extent to which they wrote against formidable racial and sexual oppressions— the material realities of life for black women in the nineteenth-century "free" states.

REPRESENTING LIES, SECRETS, AND SILENCES

The texts written by female Gothic novelists and slave narrators reflect the difficulties their authors encountered in gaining a voice in a patriarchal culture. Issues of silence and expression are central to virtually every text written by women in both genres. Observing that "the secrets of slavery are concealed like those of the Inquisition," Harriet Jacobs and her sister writers carefully showed in their texts how the

dominant discourse attempted to silence and to distort women's voices
(Jacobs 35).

As mentioned, slave narratives were almost always "framed" by
white-authored texts. This framing dramatizes the fact that slave narratives were never direct representations of reality but were mediated
in multiple ways. It was also a convention of Gothic literature from the
eighteenth century on to use various types of narrative frames. What
these frames achieve—intentionally and unintentionally—varies from
text to text. In general, the common device of framing in both Gothic
novels and slave narratives highlights the fact that we never have direct
access to the protagonist's experience. Even in an apparently immediate first-person "autobiography," as *Jane Eyre* is subtitled, the young
Jane Eyre's experiences are related through the pen of the mature
Jane Rochester.

Narrative frames call attention to the distance between reader and
protagonist. Sometimes authors explicitly encourage their readers to
work to overcome that distance. For example, in her preface to *Incidents in the Life of a Slave Girl*, Harriet Jacobs acknowledges that white
readers will find it difficult to understand "what Slavery really is. Only
by experience can any one realize how deep, and dark, and foul is that
pit of abominations" (2). Nonetheless, she states, "I do earnestly desire
to arouse the women of the North to a realizing sense of the condition
of two millions of women at the South" (1). Thus Jacobs highlights the
distance between herself and her readers but at the same time calls
forth the ideal of sisterhood—women helping other women in their
time of trouble.

Jacobs's preface is followed by an introduction written by Lydia
Maria Child. After attesting to Jacobs's integrity, Child describes the
ways Victorian ideology silences women and provides a necessary "veil"
for slavery:

> I am well aware that many will accuse me of indecorum for presenting
> these pages to the public; for the experiences of this intelligent and
> much-injured woman belong to a class which some call delicate sub-
> jects, and others indelicate. This peculiar phase of Slavery has generally
> been kept veiled; but the public ought to be made acquainted with its
> monstrous features, and I willingly take the responsibility of present-
> ing them with the veil withdrawn. I do this for the sake of my sisters
> in bondage, who are suffering wrongs so foul, that our ears are too
> delicate to listen to them. (3–4)

Child incisively describes the responsibility women have to break the silences that the patriarchal system depends on. The woman who refuses to listen to the tale of a wronged sister perpetuates the sexual double standard and thereby participates in her sister's subjugation.

Living in the deprived conditions of Haworth parsonage, Charlotte Brontë developed an unusually keen understanding of the psychological costs of being shut out from communication. In all of her writings—from her letters to M. Heger to her industrial novel *Shirley*— Brontë eloquently describes the pain that results when men refuse to communicate with the women who love them. This pain is exacerbated when women attempt to adhere to the patriarchal ideal of feminine silence. The narrator of *Shirley* states that a woman disappointed in love

> can say nothing; if she did, the result would be shame and anguish, inward remorse for self-treachery. Nature would brand such demonstration as a rebellion against her instincts, and would vindictively repay it afterwards by the thunder-bolt of self-contempt smiting suddenly in secret. Take the matter as you find it: ask no questions; utter no remonstrances: it is your best wisdom. You expected bread, and you have got a stone; break your teeth on it, and don't shriek. . . . You held out your hand for an egg, and fate put into it a scorpion. Show no consternation: close your fingers firmly upon the gift; let it sting through your palm. Never mind: in time, after your hand and arm have swelled and quivered long with torture, the squeezed scorpion will die, and you will have learned the great lesson how to endure without a sob. For the whole remnant of your life, if you survive the test—some, it is said, die under it—you will be stronger, wiser, less sensitive. Nature . . . is an excellent friend in such cases; sealing the lips, interdicting utterance, commanding a placid dissimulation. (128)

Female Gothic novelists and slave narrators constantly encounter interdictions against expressing their pain and anger. A major function of their texts is to demystify "nature," to speak the unspeakable, to give the lie to patriarchal discourse.

In *Frankenstein* Mary Shelley contrasts Walton and Frankenstein's mastery of language to the creature's exclusion from language. Both Walton and Frankenstein easily find audiences who are eager to hear their stories. Walton opens the novel by writing confidently to his sister: "You will rejoice to hear" (59). These words indicate Walton's sense of connectedness, his knowledge that expression of his thoughts and feelings is desired—indeed, eagerly anticipated—by another human being. He continues, "My first task is to assure my dear sister of my welfare" (59). For Walton, membership in a linguistic community is an unquestioned part of life, something to which he has free access.

Like Victor Frankenstein, Walton rejects the companionship of a loving woman and yearns in lonely moments for the companionship of a man. He tells his sister in his second letter that the absence of a man with whom to communicate is "a most severe evil" (63). Longing for a male companion of his race and class, he eagerly elicits conversation from Victor Frankenstein after his surprising appearance on the ship. In turn, after listening to Walton's tale, Frankenstein says, "Hear me; let me reveal my tale" (73). Through language, an immediate symbiotic connection is established between the two men. Near the end of the novel, Walton praises Frankenstein with this account of his language: "His eloquence is forcible and touching; nor can I hear him, when he relates a pathetic incident or endeavors to move the passions of pity or love, without tears" (249). Shelley repeatedly illustrates the centrality of language to human development; those people whose words are heard and credited attain power—both self-empowerment and power over others.

In contrast to Walton and Frankenstein's development, a striking aspect of the development of Shelley's unnamed creature is his exclusion from linguistic communities. Because of his freakish appearance, the creature is labeled monstrous, frightening, other, and—most importantly—he is denied a voice. All of his violent actions result from his desire to be heard, his desperation to make Frankenstein listen to him. Over and over, he pleads with his creator: "How can I move thee? Will no intreaties cause thee to turn a favourable eye upon thy creature? . . . Listen to my tale . . . But hear me. . . . Listen to me, Frankenstein . . . listen to me. . . . Still canst thou listen to me and grant me thy compassion. . . . Hear my tale" (142–43). Frankenstein finally listens and for a brief (but very brief) moment is moved by the creature's words. Mary Shelley places the creature's words at the center of the novel to emphasize their central importance to her story. In this way, Shelley's myth of origins departs radically from the Biblical myth of origins, in which the voice of Eve is absent. Giving the creature space to speak also enables Shelley to gain revenge for summer evenings in Switzerland in 1816 when she quietly listened as Lord Byron, Percy Shelley, John Polidori, and M. G. Lewis told ghost stories representing women as villains and victims.[21]

In *Frankenstein*, Mary Shelley attempts to give voice to those people in society who are traditionally removed from the centers of linguistic power, people who are defined as alien, inferior, or monstrous solely because of physical features (such as sex or race) or material conditions (such as poverty). Shelley's creature intuits the dialogical principle that Bakhtin describes: "The word in language is half someone else's. . . . It exists in other people's mouths, in other people's contexts, serving other people's intentions: it is from there that one must take the word, and make it one's own" (Bakhtin 293–94). The creature attempts to "populate" language "with his own intention, his own accent" (Bakhtin 293). Excluded from dialogue, however, he finds that he cannot easily appropriate language; he cannot seize and transform it into his "private property: many words stubbornly resist, others remain alien, sound foreign in the mouth of the one who appropriated them and who now speaks them; they cannot be assimilated into his context" (Bakhtin 294). The creature remains isolated because Victor Frankenstein, determined to justify his own behavior, hardens his heart against the voice of the other. He disallows the creature's interpretation of events and denies his requests for the basic human necessities of companionship and language. Echoing God's warning to Adam not to listen to Satan, Frankenstein warns Walton not to listen to the "monster": "He is eloquent and persuasive . . . but trust him not. His soul is as hellish as his form, full of treachery and fiendlike malice. Hear him not" (248).

Emily Brontë's *Wuthering Heights* is similar to *Frankenstein* in its use of narrative frames that dramatize the exclusion of Catherine and Heathcliff from the dominant discourse. Just as Shelley emphasizes the marginalization of her creature's voice, Brontë gives readers only momentary glimpses into Catherine's and Heathcliff's stories, always mediated by the narrative voices of Lockwood and Nelly Dean. Echoing Milton's God and Shelley's Frankenstein, Isabella warns Nelly not to listen to Heathcliff: "Don't put faith in a single word he speaks. He's a lying fiend! a monster, and not a human being!" (188). As readers, however, we grow increasingly suspicious of the words of the narrators (Walton, Frankenstein, Lockwood, and Nelly Dean) as they are shown to be self-deluded, self-interested, morally blind, and occasionally stupid. Nelly, the voice of English convention and repression, uses silence to prevent Catherine and Heathcliff from reaching understanding. Her unscrupulous eavesdropping and partial revelations (half-truths) precipitate Catherine's death. Yet not even Nelly

Dean and Lockwood can completely silence the stories they want to re-press. Like Frankenstein's creature, Heathcliff is eloquent and moving in key passages, especially as his death approaches. Mary Shelley and Emily Brontë understood that the stories of social aliens are always mediated by the voices of the dominant culture. Nonetheless, both authors suggest that the ghosts of subversive stories will survive and even prosper subterraneously.

In 1892, the African American essayist Anna Julia Cooper wrote an eloquent apology for women breaking silence: "It is not the intelligent woman vs. the ignorant woman; nor the white woman vs. the black, the brown, and the red,—it is not even the cause of woman vs. man. Nay, 'tis woman's strongest vindication for speaking that *the world needs to hear her voice*. It would be subversive of every human interest that the cry of one-half the human family be stifled. . . . Hers is every interest that has lacked an interpreter and a defender. Her cause is linked with that of every agony that has been dumb—every wrong that needs a voice" (121–22). Women's Gothic novels and slave narratives forcefully dramatize the solidarity that Cooper describes between "the Wrongs of Woman" (as Wollstonecraft put it) and the agony of all people who have been rendered dumb in a classist, racist, patriarchal society.

2
LABYRINTHS
OF
TERROR

ALTHOUGH Gothic novels and slave narratives were written within the very different literary conventions of fantasy and "facticity," both genres focus on horrifying aspects of patriarchal cultures. Through looking squarely at the horrors that confronted them, female Gothic novelists and slave narrators were able to develop incisive analyses of the forces of oppression within their societies. They represented the corruption produced by the dominant ideology as all-pervasive: every person and every place is infected by the poison of patriarchal, racist, or classist discourse.

Many nineteenth-century readers recognized similarities between the Gothic and slave narrative texts. The feminist-abolitionist Angelina Grimké expressed a common interpretation of slave narratives when she stated in 1838, "Many and many a tale of romantic horror can the slaves tell" (qtd. in Sekora, "Black Message" 498). Because the tales told by slave narrators and female Gothic novelists included scenes of violence and sexual sadism, writers of both genres sometimes felt compelled to defend themselves against charges that they were writing sensationalistic or pornographic tales.

Ann Radcliffe defended the morality of her writing by distinguishing it from other types of Gothic fiction. She reacted against the tales of romantic horror written by men like M. G. Lewis by asserting that she wrote tales of terror, not horror. In her article "On the Supernatural in Poetry," she argued that "terror and horror are so far opposite, that the first expands the soul, and awakens the faculties to a high degree of life; the other contracts, freezes, and nearly annihilates them" (150). In tales of terror, she continued, "the dreaded evil" is "uncertain" and "obscure" (151); the imagination of the protagonist and the readers is awakened and they may be stimulated to positive action. In this way, terror may be life-affirming and liberating, whereas horror is paralyzing and deadly.

Because slave narratives told shocking stories about slaveholders' cruelties and perversities, critics often accused the writers and publishers of catering to pornographic tastes. Many of the narratives written before 1830 were in fact tales of adventure and criminality that probably appealed to the type of audience that enjoyed Lewisite Gothic. For example, the narrative of Briton Hammon (1760), "usually considered the first by an American slave," was "dictated to an amanuensis-editor who shape[d] it into the popular form of captivity narrative" (Sekora, "Black Message" 486). The white editor depicts Hammon as being delighted to return to "his good old Master" after being captured by Indians and witnessing their "horrid Cruelty and inhuman Barbarity" (qtd. in Sekora, "Black Message" 486). Other popular narratives purported to record the dying confessions of "mad" black criminals and were published after the "criminals'" executions. Far from challenging slavery, these narratives represented "white institutions [as] divinely ordained as well as omnipotent. It is precisely the 'insanity' of rebellion against such power that editors inscribed" (Sekora, "Black Message" 491).

In contrast to these early narratives, the narratives solicited by abolitionists exposed the horrors of slavery with the goal of ending them. If Radcliffe wrote her stories to "awaken" her readers and inspire them to resistance, abolitionist slave narrators were even more committed to rousing their audience to action. In the words of Frederick Douglass, "to expose [slavery] is to kill it." Unfortunately, people who identify problems are often accused of creating them. As a consequence, people who fight for human liberation often need to defend themselves against the suggestion that perversity exists in their own psyche rather than in social reality. John Sekora notes that "when white editors like [Theodore and Angelina] Weld were criticized for horror-hunting and sensation-seeking, they replied that southerners themselves retailed atrocity stories and that slavery was innately horrible. 'Abolitionists exaggerate the horrors of slavery? Impossible! They have never conceived half its horrors!' was [William Lloyd] Garrison's response" ("Black Message" 501). A similar point can be made about female Gothic writing: women described their terror not because they took some kind of sado-masochistic pleasure from contemplating violence, perversion, and suffering but because they were attempting to understand their pain and to transform their worlds. They employed their imaginations not to *invent* but to *identify* sources of terror.

The psychoanalyst Alice Miller has shown that any dominant ideology's most powerful message to its oppressed is "thou shalt not be aware." [1] Thus the most fundamental acts of revolution involve claiming knowledge and naming the sources of oppression—acts which require a great amount of imaginative energy precisely because the dominant ideology mystifies power relations in complex, insidious ways. The female authors of Gothic novels and slave narratives described three primary sources of terror and horror in their lives. First, they emphasized the terrifying aspects of the patriarchal family and depicted patriarchs as parasites who prey on the sexual, emotional, reproductive, and economic resources of women. Second, they insisted that *all* of society—from intimate family relationships to large state institutions—is corrupted by perverse power inequities. Third, they dramatized the means by which people in positions of power attempt to deprive subjugated peoples of the power to know.

THE PATRIARCHAL FAMILY

The institution of the patriarchal family in Europe and the United States provided the social and psychological foundation for most of the injustice and cruelty described in slave narratives and female Gothic novels. The hierarchy of the family reflects and supports the hierarchies of the state: the male head holds all real power; the wife is both the victim and the mediator of his power; children, servants, slaves, animals, and all the riches of the earth are viewed as resources to be tamed and exploited for the patriarch's convenience and pleasure. When this system functions smoothly, whoever and whatever cannot be tamed is destroyed ("savage" human beings are annihilated, wild animals are hunted, rain forests are ravaged, and so on).

Fortunately, as Foucault has said, "Where there is power, there is resistance" (95). The patriarch's power is never as complete as he wants it to be. Recognizing that patriarchal power is not absolute, female authors of Gothic novels and slave narratives did what they could to dissect and disrupt the functioning of the patriarchal family and state. One of their first tasks was to attack the institutionalization of sexuality and reproduction. The institution of marriage was a primary target for the middle-class authors of Gothic novels, whereas the southern institution of raping and breeding enslaved women was a primary target for the authors of slave narratives.

At the beginning of the eighteenth century Mary Astell described marriage as an institution of slavery, and at the end of the century Mary Wollstonecraft reached the same conclusion. Recent feminist scholars have confirmed Astell's and Wollstonecraft's analyses. Mary Poovey summarizes the legal subjection of women in eighteenth-century England: "From the laws of strict entail, which awarded the entire patriarchal estate to the eldest son, to the Matrimonial Act of 1770, which prosecuted as witches 'all women . . . that shall . . . impose upon, seduce, and betray into matrimony any of His Majesty's subjects by means of scent, paints, . . . false hair, . . . high-heeled shoes, or bolstered hips,' women were legally 'cyphers,' prohibited from political and economic activity except through the agency of a legal 'subject,' man" (*The Proper Lady* x). In *Feminism in Eighteenth-Century England*, Katharine Rogers argues that changes in attitudes about marriage both improved and worsened the situation of English women in the eighteenth century. On the one hand, many men began to view women as potentially intelligent companions who should be married for love as much as for convenience, position, and money. On the other hand, "the persisting patriarchal institutions gained emotional force when women were supposed to be bound to their husbands by love more than law" (1). For women, the daily conditions of marriage continued to range "from mild subjection to virtual slavery. Legally, man and wife were considered one person—in effect, of course, the man" (7).

On the other side of the ocean, participants in the first American women's rights convention, held in July 1848 in Seneca Falls, New York, affirmed the analyses of English feminists. They declared in their "history of repeated injuries and usurpations on the part of man toward woman" that man has made woman, "if married, in the eye of the law, civilly dead" ("Declaration of Sentiments" 193). The oppression that these nineteenth-century activists described as "civil death" is similar to the state Patterson describes as "social death."

In *Reconstructing Womanhood* Hazel Carby describes significant differences between the ways black women's and white women's bodies were co-opted and their sexuality institutionalized under southern slavery. The black woman's "reproductive destiny was bound to capital accumulation; black women gave birth to property and, directly, to capital itself in the form of slaves, and all slaves inherited their status from their mothers" (25). In contrast, white women gave birth to "the inheritors of that property" (24). Furthermore, Carby points out, "The effect of black female sexuality on the white male was represented in an entirely different form from that of the figurative power of white female sexuality. Confronted by the black woman, the white man behaved in a manner that was considered to be entirely untempered by any virtuous qualities; the white male, in fact, was represented as being merely prey to the rampant sexuality of his female slaves" (27). The idea that men are "merely prey to the rampant sexuality" of women has a long history in Western thought. As feminists have long noted, throughout church history the dominant ideology has cast Woman into two inhuman roles: Eve, the mother of sin and sexuality, and Madonna, the Virgin Mother of God. The enslavement of Africans made it profitable for white men to divide their conflicting notions of Woman into stereotypes of good white angels and evil black beasts.

While middle-class white women were idealized by the "cult of true womanhood" and the concept of the angel in the house, black women were demonized as subhuman chattel and whores. These concepts were interdependent. As Carby argues, "In order to perceive the cultural effectivity of ideologies of black female sexuality, it is necessary to consider the determining force of ideologies of white female sexuality: stereotypes only appear to exist in isolation while actually depending on a nexus of figurations which can be explained only in relation to each other" (20). The ideological system reflected and reproduced white men's confusion about the "nature" of Woman and Black, but the system consistently upheld the right of white men to control *all* women's sexuality and reproduction. In *Within the Plantation Household* Elizabeth Fox-Genovese shows that "slavery as a social system shaped the experience of all its women" (38). In households where the angel-whore dichotomy was clearly maintained, wives were expected to be asexual and to be content while their husbands vented their "animal lusts" on black women. As a result of these rigid, dehumanizing stereotypes, all women were denied dignified, free heterosexual expression; heterosexuality was fundamentally connected to violence, coercion, deception, and betrayal.

In some cases, white southern men chose to make explicit the historical connection between marriage and slavery. Louisa Picquet's narrative, recorded by the Methodist minister Hiram Mattison, describes the long history of the enforced "concubinage" of both Louisa and her mother. Louisa's father, Mr. Randolph, impregnates and then sells Louisa's fifteen-year-old mother. Mr. Cook, their new owner, appar-

ently fathers three children by Louisa's mother and attempts to force
the adolescent Louisa to have sex with him. Louisa is purchased when
she is fourteen years old by a fifty-year-old white man, Mr. Williams,
who intends to use her as a wife: a sexual partner, housekeeper, care-
taker of his present children, and mother of his future children. He is
not rich; he has to borrow money from his brother to buy a slave-wife.
Picquet cites multiple examples of rich and poor men who bought
women to use as wives.

The relationship between Picquet and Williams is similar in many
respects to a traditional marriage; indeed, at Williams's funeral, Picquet is addressed by the minister as Williams's wife. Williams is obses-
sively jealous and possessive of Picquet: "He never ha[d] no gentlemen
company home. Sometimes . . . if I did not let him in [the house] in a
minute, when I would be asleep, he'd come in and take the light, and
look under the bed, and in the wardrobe, and all over, and then ask
me why I did not let him in sooner. I did not know what it meant till I
learnt his ways" (19). The young girl asks to be sold, but "he got awful
mad, and said nothin' but death should separate us"—a ghastly cari-
cature of marriage vows (19–20). Like many husbands who terrorize
their wives, Williams threatens to "blow [her] brains out" if she runs
away. Picquet is forced to live with him for many years and to give
birth four times. Without any human help to hope for, Picquet turns
to prayer. She uses her knowledge that the Bible forbids "adultery"
and "livin' in sin" as a justification for praying for Williams's death: if
God "would just take [Williams] out of the way, I'd get religion and be
true to Him as long as I lived" (22).

When Williams finally gets sick, Picquet says, "He begin to get good,
and talked kind to me" (22). He promises to free her and her children
after his death if she will promise to go to New York, and he leaves his
few possessions to her. Picquet is not impressed by his "kindness"; unlike many legally married middle-class wives, she has no sentimental
notions about her state of exploitation. After Williams dies, she says,
"I didn't cry nor nothin', for I was glad he was dead; for I thought I
could have some peace and happiness then. I was left *free,* and that
made me so glad I could hardly believe it myself" (23). Picquet's freedom has multivalent meanings: her joy is the joy of a slave who is "free
at last!" and it is also the joy of an abused "wife" whose husband's
death renders her "Free! Body and soul free!", in the words of Kate
Chopin (78).

Although Picquet's narrative was recorded by a rather obtuse, lecherous white male pastor, her incisive sense of humor and remarkable flair for upsetting the expectations of her white audience are strongly evident in the text. She pointedly observes that before his death Williams offered her abundant advice on "how to conduct myself." Because she is very light-skinned, Williams tells her "not to let any one know who I was, or that I was colored . . . and, if I conducted myself right, some one would want to marry me" (23). Picquet responds to his advice as follows: she moves to Cincinnati instead of New York, marries a black man instead of a white man (and notes that their "darkest" child is also their "smartest"), publishes a narrative telling the world who she is and where she came from, and devotes her energy to rescuing her mother from slavery.

Female Gothic heroines are never forced to endure the amount of physical exploitation and abuse that enslaved protagonists confront, but Gothic novels are actually more pessimistic than slave narratives about their protagonists' chances for triumphing against patriarchal strictures. Part of the difference stems from the fact that Gothic novels suffer (however rebelliously) from the constraints of sentimental fiction; heroines are trapped within a genre that allows them to be objects of interest only so long as they are young and virtuous. In contrast, the authors of slave narratives can participate in a long literary history of slave rebellions in which protagonists are valued for their intelligence, endurance, and rage.[2] Many critics have noted that Harriet Jacobs was influenced by the conventions of sentimental fiction, but her narrative departs from the sentimental genre in that all of her hopes for a freely chosen egalitarian marriage are destroyed in the first chapters of the book and in the remainder of the book she struggles more for freedom and revenge than for love. Her enemy is clearly identified, and her objectives are unambiguous. Like Louisa Picquet, Jacobs is horribly victimized, but, also like Picquet, she triumphs to a large extent over her archenemy.

Because the forces that oppress white middle-class women are usually mystified and subterranean, female Gothic heroines are usually more confused by their oppression than the protagonists of slave narratives are. Their labyrinths of terror may not be as complex and gruesome as the labyrinths of southern slavery, but the heroines cannot discern the pattern as clearly. They often end up trapped in the maze of compulsory heterosexuality.[3]

In her depiction of the relationship between Shirley Keeldar and Louis Moore in *Shirley*, Charlotte Brontë articulated unusually clear insights into the sado-masochistic implications of the type of love valorized in patriarchal ideology. Shirley and Louis are social rebels inasmuch as their union violates class codes. Shirley has more money and higher social status than Louis, and she believes their union could be subversive. Louis, however, resents her money and power because he wants unquestioned dominance over her, as the following interchange demonstrates:

> "Are we equal then, sir? Are we equal at last?" [asks Shirley].
> "You are younger, frailer, feebler, more ignorant than I" [replies Louis].
> "Will you be good to me, and never tyrannize? . . . You name me leopardess: remember, the leopardess is tameless," said she.
> "Tame or fierce, wild or subdued, you are *mine*." (579)

Shirley longs for an egalitarian relationship while Louis desires conquest. In his journal, he repeatedly describes Shirley as a wild beast that he wants to tame: "Panthress!—beautiful forest-born!—wily, tameless, peerless nature! She gnaws her chain: I see the white teeth working at the steel! She has dreams of her wild woods, and pinings after virgin freedom. I wish Sympson [Shirley's uncle] would come again, and oblige her again to entwine her arms about me" (584). Louis's reference to Sympson shows that he understands that Shirley's concession to marry him is motivated largely by her desire to escape from her uncle's control. As Shirley's closest male relative, Sympson has always tried to tell her how to dispose of her money and time. She decides to marry outside her class in order to declare her contempt for social conventions and, in particular, her independence from her uncle's will. Having consented to marry Louis, she postpones their marriage as long as possible, realizing that marriage for women is another form of acquiescence to male domination. As Louis says, she "gnaws her chain," but she finally is unable to find a way to live free from men's control. Her only freedom lies in her ability to choose a different master.

Unlike Shirley, Louisa Picquet is remarkably successful in achieving the freedom of body and soul that all enslaved protagonists and female Gothic heroines seek. The two genres show, however, that enslaved women and nominally free women usually encounter somewhat different obstacles in their fight for liberation. The oppression of the former group is blatant, violent, and publicly sanctioned; the oppression of the latter is subterranean, disguised, and mystified. In general, slave narratives represent protagonists as facing a greater battle in attempting to liberate their bodies than their souls; Picquet, for example, never represents herself as feeling emotionally bound to Williams or to her other oppressors. In contrast, female Gothic novels represent heroines as facing a greater battle in attempting to liberate their souls than their bodies; the romanticization of compulsory heterosexuality often binds women to their oppressors even when they are legally free, as Charlotte Brontë's novels clearly demonstrate.

Ultimately, the protagonists in both genres are attacked at every level; their minds and bodies are constantly subjected to assault and colonization. Nonetheless, the different historical circumstances elicit different responses for the heroines who are fighting for their freedom. In particular, marriage offers various dangers and possibilities. For female Gothic heroines, marriage is typically a capitulation to men's control, whereas for enslaved protagonists, marriage is often a courageous act of humanity and rebellion. The differences stem from the laws that regulated white women and black people: marriage was a means of legally rendering white women nonexistent (making them "one" with their husbands), whereas marriage between slaves and between a slave and a free black was forbidden because it would demonstrate their humanity and give them legal claims on one another. Advocates of slavery, attempting to justify their desire for total control over the bodies of slaves, argued that slaves were incapable of sustaining affectionate relationships among themselves.

In *Wuthering Heights*, Emily Brontë develops a thoroughly unsentimental analysis of bourgeois ideas about marriage and the family. Brontë uses the character of Isabella in particular to attack literary representations of innocent, naive heroines, such as the original Gothic heroine, Isabella of Otranto. Through Isabella, Brontë deconstructs "femininity": Isabella is willful, spoiled, and stupid rather than innocently and virtuously naive. Isabella's stubborn clinging to romantic notions about Heathcliff and marriage is an effective representation of the peculiar human ability to sustain a consciousness totally disconnected from rational evidence.

Isabella's marriage to Heathcliff is not, however, an unmitigated disaster; for her, it is more educational than tragic—a point that critics consistently overlook. Gilbert and Gubar, for instance, argue that after Isabella escapes from the Heights, she is exiled from the book and might as well be dead. What they fail to see is that rather than simply constricting Isabella, Heathcliff's forthright violence and cruelty unmask the tyranny at the base of every other marriage in the book. When the garb of respectability is ripped away, Isabella is psychologically freed to escape from her husband and to live for another thirteen years, much longer than any other woman in the novel survives marriage. Catherine's union with Edgar is more disastrous because Edgar's tyranny is more insidious. Heathcliff is utterly contemptuous of Isabella, but he does not need to control her or to keep her around to prove his manhood; therefore, he does not pursue or torment her after she leaves. Edgar, the polite conventionalist, seems to care little more for his sister than Heathcliff does; he apparently makes no attempt to see or to help her, interested finally (like Heathcliff) only in the son and heir she has produced.

Few female Gothic novelists were as consistently critical of the institution of marriage as Emily Brontë. However, no well-known Gothic novel written by an English woman between 1790 and 1865 presents its readers with a sustained picture of a happy marriage or a happy heterosexual relationship of any kind. Happy wives rarely appear in Gothic novels; when they are represented at all, they die quickly. Occasionally the conclusion of a Gothic novel promises future wedded bliss for the heroine, but that marriage is never represented within the text.

Similarly, the authors of slave narratives sometimes mention good marriages, but they do not describe them in detail. In general, female Gothic novels and slave narratives distinguish between the institutionalization of sexuality (in marriage, rape, and breeding) and genuine human affection and nurturance. Slavery in the United States and compulsory heterosexuality in England corrupted every aspect of life and exacted a price of every relationship. Nonetheless, protagonists in both genres attempt to find a type of love—love between women; love between mothers and children; love across lines of class, race, or ethnicity; or love among slaves—that could enable them to subvert the dominant order and to find sexual-emotional fulfillment.

When enslaved people married, they asserted their humanity, resisted despair, and defied the slaveholder's control. When they allowed themselves to love, however, they became extremely vulnerable, because enslaved husbands, wives, and children had no legal control over their futures. Furthermore, even when slaves successfully demanded the right to choose a partner, they were denied the basic resources needed to sustain intimacy: time, privacy, and space. Toni Morrison points to this deprivation in *Beloved*, in the relationship between Sethe and Halle. Conditions conducive to pleasure do not exist: Sethe is laughed at by her "good" mistress because she desires a ceremony to mark her union with Halle, and when Sethe and Halle attempt to find privacy for lovemaking in the cornfields, they get instead "public display" (26). Despite these humiliations, Morrison portrays Sethe and Halle as luckier than most slaves. For a short period of time, they are allowed to choose each other, Halle's sex is not rented out, and Sethe is not raped.

William Wells Brown's narrative portrays intense emotional attachments among enslaved people, but he also emphasizes the high price slaves pay for loving. He supports his thesis that "there are no good masters" by showing that even relatively decent slaveholders use slaves' emotional attachments to strengthen their control over the slaves' lives (203). His last mistress, Mrs. Price, is "very proud of her servants, always keeping them well dressed" (212). She is "determined" to get Brown married. When he shows no interest in her slave girl, Maria, Mrs. Price invites Brown into her room, "telling me to take a chair and sit down. I did so, thinking it rather strange, for servants are not very often asked thus to sit down in the same room with the master or mistress. She said that she had found out that I did not care enough about Maria to marry her. I told her that was true. She then asked me if there was a girl in the city that I loved. Well, now, this was coming into too close quarters with me! People, generally, don't like to tell their love stories to everybody that think fit to ask about them" (213). Far from feeling flattered by Mrs. Price's attention, Brown feels violated by her prying questions. Remarkably clearheaded, he sees her patronizing kindness as a "trap laid . . . to make me satisfied with my new home" (213).

Mrs. Price manages to discover that Brown is interested in a woman named Eliza, and she purchases Eliza in hopes that the two will marry. Brown, however, understands that an emotional commitment to Eliza would make him doubly vulnerable. First, caring for her would make it more difficult for him to run away. Second, the "marriage" would have no legal basis; they could be separated at any time at the whim of their owners. With wonderful wit and foresight, Brown avoids marriage and maneuvers himself into a situation where he can escape.

Because of the multitudinous difficulties, love and marriage were almost invariably ill fated for slaves. The young Louisa Picquet is separated from a man whom she "likes very well" and who wants to marry her because he decides to run away and she is afraid to go along. Mary Prince, a West Indian slave whose ghostwritten narrative was first published in 1831, was more fortunate than Picquet in that she managed to marry the man she loved. However, when her owner, Mr. Wood, "heard of my marriage, he flew into a great rage, and . . . Mrs. Wood was [even] more vexed about my marriage than her husband. She could not forgive me for getting married, but stirred up Mr. Wood to flog me dreadfully with the horsewhip. . . . She said that she would not have nigger men about the yards and premises" (17–18). Prince is harshly abused because her decision to marry is seen by her owners as an unforgivable act of self-assertion and humanity. She observes that "I had not much happiness in my marriage, owing to my being a slave. It made my husband sad to see me so ill-treated" (18). She eventually gains her freedom during a trip with the Woods to England, but part of the price of her freedom is a permanent separation from her husband, who is trapped in the West Indies. If she returns to him there, she will be reenslaved.

When Harriet Jacobs is young, she becomes attached to "a young colored carpenter; a free born man" (37). They plan to marry, but when the perversely jealous Dr. Flint learns of their relationship, he beats Jacobs and threatens to imprison or kill her. He declares, "If I ever know of your speaking to him, I will cowhide you both; and if I catch him lurking about my premises, I will shoot him as soon as I would a dog" (40). Contemplating this situation many years later, Jacobs expresses a sentiment often felt by enslaved people: "Why does the slave ever love? Why allow the tendrils of the heart to twine around objects which may at any moment be wrenched away by the hand of violence?" (37).

Few slave narratives depict much happiness coming from emotional connections among slaves in the South. Nonetheless, as Orlando Patterson observes, slaves continued to defy their dehumanization by valuing each other:

> Against all odds [the slave] strove for some measure of regularity and predictability in his [*sic*] social life. Because his kin relations were illegitimate, they were all the more cherished. Because he was considered degraded, he was all the more infused with the yearning for dignity. Because of his formal isolation and liminality, he was acutely sensitive to the realities of community. The fierce love of the slave mother for her child is attested in every slaveholding society; everywhere the slave's zest for life and fellowship confounded the slaveholder class. (337–38)

In the context of slavery, every effort slaves made to maintain relationships with other slaves was an act of resistance. Consequently, slave narratives usually represent family relationships among slaves as filled with tenderness, passion, and loyalty.

In contrast, black women in the "free" North usually represented their own marriages and the marriages of their mothers as plagued by the same type of abuse that white women had been describing for centuries. For black women, enslavement by whites often was replaced by subjugation to their own men. Nancy Prince, whose narrative was originally published in 1850, was the granddaughter of an enslaved African who "fought for liberty" in the American Revolution and his Indian wife, who was enslaved by the English (5). Although nominally free as a child in Massachussetts, Prince witnessed many incidents of enslavement, racism, and destitution. Her narrative expresses outrage against these injustices, but she portrays her stepfather as the bane of her childhood, recalling that she and her siblings were severely abused by him. After his death or disappearance, Prince says that "mother chose to marry again; this was like death to us all" (18). The new father figure is as bad as his predecessor; he is violent and "very cross," and he expects to be supported financially by his stepchildren (18–19).

The Memoir of Mrs. Chloe Spear, written by a "Lady of Boston" in 1832, describes another typical marriage situation. Chloe Spear, an intelligent, resourceful woman, was born in Africa in 1750 and sold in Boston as a child. She is set free with her husband and child, only to find a new type of servitude:

> After returning from a hard day's work [as a washerwoman], she many a time, went to washing for her customers in the night, while her husband was taking his rest . . . then arose, prepared breakfast and went out to work again, leaving her ironing to be done on her return at night. Cesar [her husband], having been accustomed to cooking, &c. could, on these occasions, wait upon himself and boarders, during her absence; but was quite willing she should make ready a good supper, after she came home.
>
> Her husband was fond of finery and show, and would sometimes say to her, "Chloe, why don't you wear silk gown, dress up smart, like udder colour women?" (Sterling 92)

This narrative represents Chloe as suffering not only from enslavement and racism but also from the mundane injustice of marriage. Despite everything, she slowly, secretly manages to save enough money to buy an unfinished house, only to find that "the purchase must be made in her husband's name, 'cause he de *head*'" (Sterling 93). Undaunted, Chloe convinces Cesar to buy the house, and before her death in 1815 she builds a considerable estate.

Like enslaved protagonists, most Gothic heroines are separated from the men they love by a perverse patriarch such as Montoni or General Tilney. In early Gothic texts, heroines struggle bravely to be reunited with their true love, and they usually succeed—only to find that their true love is becoming a patriarch himself. Henry Tilney, for example, becomes almost as authoritarian as his father in *Northanger Abbey*. Between 1819 and 1865, this pattern varies. In *Mathilda*, Mary Shelley's novella about incest, Mathilda's lover is literally her perverse father; in *Wuthering Heights*, Heathcliff acquires patriarchal characteristics after being rejected rather than after being accepted by the heroine; and in *Jane Eyre*, Rochester is simultaneously Jane's beloved and the patriarch who separates her from the man she loves. Later nineteenth-century female Gothic tales like "The Yellow Wallpaper" often follow the pattern of *Jane Eyre*: the frightening patriarch *is* the lover or husband. In twentieth-century mass-produced Gothics, this pattern becomes formulaic; the heroine fears that "somebody's trying to kill me, and I think it's my husband" (Russ 32).[4] In all the variations, female Gothic novelists persistently suggest that heterosexuality in patriarchal cultures is intricately connected to coercion and violence.

Female Gothic novels and slave narratives both suggest that the violence that maintains the hierarchical relationship between husband and wife is reproduced in relationships between (white) parents and children. As Mary Wollstonecraft put it, "Parents often love their children in the most brutal manner" and embitter their children's lives "by the most despotic stretch of power" (*A Vindication* 150). Wollstonecraft was well aware that the subjugation of women was fundamentally connected to the subjugation of children and slaves: "obedience, unconditional obedience, is the catch-word of tyrants of every description," she argued, "and . . . one kind of despotism supports another" (150).

Gothic novelists demonstrated in both their lives and their fiction the connections between their abuse as children and their bondage to patriarchal ideology as adults. Time and again, Charlotte Brontë attempted to compensate for the absence of fatherly love by providing her heroines with a teacher-lover, an older, wiser man who would nurture the heroine emotionally and encourage her to grow intellectually. This obsession was, of course, based on Brontë's profound emotional deprivation in childhood and her lifelong frustrating relationships with her father, her brother, and M. Heger, her Brussels schoolmaster. In *Jane Eyre* Brontë attempts simultaneously to satisfy Jane's regressive desire for a father-master and her feminist desire for a lover who is a friend and an equal. As long as Rochester is Jane's employer, the power imbalance in their relationship is similar to that of a parent and a child. Through the course of the novel Brontë attempts to equalize the relationship but she can never quite imagine a father figure becoming an equal. When Jane marries Rochester, she actually assumes the role of a parent, taking care of the physically crippled Rochester. This is a typical pattern that serves the needs of a patriarchal culture; women are coerced into serving the needs of men out of their own desperate need for the emotional sustenance that is constantly promised but never granted. The successfully socialized woman will attempt to meet her own needs by "mothering" her husband and, in many cases, her own father.

Thus Jane Eyre falls in love with her (deceitful) employer and Lucy Snowe with her (cruel) teacher. In *Villette* Brontë makes the basis of patriarchal sexuality explicit when Polly Home transfers her love for her father to Graham Bretton. Polly has the crucial resources (beauty, money, and cultivated stupidity) to attract Graham. Brontë shows that Polly's "good fortune" in finding an "ideal" love is precisely what reduces her to a perpetually dependent, childish state. Because Graham is the ideal patriarch (paternalistic kindness masks his domination), he will "shelter" and "protect" Polly, and she will be his little mother. After Lucy Snowe has gained some freedom from the mystifications of romance, she pities Polly rather than envying her.

In contrast to her feelings for Polly, Lucy is strongly and unwillingly attracted to Ginevra Fanshawe, one of those rare women who somehow manage *not* to internalize the feminine ideal of self-sacrificial love. Ginevra loves not a patriarch but a foppish clown who is her social and intellectual equal. She successfully sabotages the system, scorning "good" young men and celebrating the physical charms of the man of her choice. Ginevra's self-confident clarity about her own tastes and desires and her apparent immunity to the dispersions of society dazzle Lucy and inspire her to assert herself, to express her desire for Paul Emanuel.

The goal of physical and intellectual liberation required Gothic heroines to search for ways to preserve their dignity while also finding sexual and emotional fulfillment, but the novels are not optimistic about the possibilities. Slave narratives are even less optimistic about the possibilities of protagonists finding love and sexual fulfillment. Furthermore, the protagonists in both genres face a variety of assaults on their bodies and minds from forces outside the family.

ALL-PERVADING CORRUPTION

The perversions in the patriarchal family reflected and reproduced perversions throughout society. Between 1790 and 1865 many people in Britain and the United States debated issues concerning human liberation, and they appeared eager to read stories by and about women, workers, slaves, and colonized peoples. However, as John Sekora has noted, the controversies were usually between competing master texts of English and American history, "each armed with formidable institutional accoutrements" ("Black Message" 493). Most privileged people did not actually want to know how oppression worked; therefore, they cultivated "a habitual attitude of disbelief toward black [and female and working-class and children's] accounts" of their own experience (497).

Advocates of slavery argued that the patriarchal system was good for everyone: slaves were as happy as they could be, and slaveholders were taking care of their God-given responsibilities. Any problems were the fault of a few unusual individuals. Similar arguments were constructed by defenders of traditional marriage: wives were happiest when they submitted to their husbands, and husbands had the God-given duty to be the heads of their households. When slaves and wives encountered an "occasionally" unjust master, they were commanded to submit patiently in order to uphold the God-ordained social order. By promoting the idea that suffering for God is good for the soul, the New Testament provided ideological justification for oppressors to continue oppressing and victims to accept abuse: "Slaves, submit yourselves to your masters with all respect, not only to those who are good and considerate, but also to those who are harsh. For it is commendable if a man bears up under the pain of unjust suffering because he is conscious of God. But how is it to your credit if you receive a beating for doing wrong and endure it? But if you suffer for doing good and you endure it, this is commendable before God" (1 Pet. 2.18–20).

The authors of slave narratives and female Gothic novels responded to this ideological assault by representing the social system as thoroughly corrupt. Their texts emphasize that "no pen can give an adequate description of the all-pervading corruption produced by slavery" (Jacobs 51). Protagonists often flee from abusive situations only to find their new circumstances even more threatening. Louisa Picquet, for example, stated, "I was glad when I heard I was taken off to be sold, because of what I escape; but I jump out of the fryin'-pan into the fire" (15). Slave narratives emphasize that the exception to the rule is not a perverse master but a kind one—and he or she soon will be corrupted or killed by the system. Harriet Jacobs observes that "slavery is a curse to the whites as well as to the blacks. It makes white fathers cruel and sensual; the sons violent and licentious; it contaminates the daughters, and makes the wives wretched. And as for the colored race, it needs an abler pen than mine to describe the extremity of their sufferings" (52). Similarly, Frederick Douglass argues that "the slaveholder, as well as the slave, is the victim of the slave system. A man's character greatly takes its hue and shape from the form and color of things about him. Under the whole heavens there is no relation more unfavorable to the development of honorable character, than that sustained by the slaveholder to the slave" (*My Bondage* 54). Douglass supports this analysis with a description of a white woman who, as long as she "depended almost entirely upon her own industry for a living," was "of an excellent disposition, kind, gentle and cheerful" (90). After she becomes a slaveholder, however, "the fatal poison of irresponsible power" transforms her "noble nature" into "fretful bitterness" (92). "Slavery," Douglass observes, "can change a saint into a sinner, and an angel into a demon" (90). He indicts the social system but does not deny individual responsibility. In one of the most insightful passages in *My Bondage and My Freedom*, Douglass observes: "The slave is a subject, subjected by others; the slaveholder is a subject, but he is the author of his own subjection" (69).

Because slaves were usually kept in a state of abysmal ignorance about politics and geography, many did not know that "free" states existed, and few knew how to get north. Douglass points out that those slaves who attempted to flee north "did more than Patrick Henry, when he resolved upon liberty or death. With us it was a doubtful liberty at most, and almost certain death if we failed" (*Narrative* 118). For those slaves who were subjected to torture daily, the only hope of a better life was to find a better master. Time and again, however, slaves' hopes were shattered; slavery did not produce good masters. Instead of improved conditions, most slaves gained from new masters an education they never wanted: first-hand knowledge of the multitudinous ways one human being can inflict pain on another. Mary Prince's story is a representative example: "I hoped, when I left Capt. I——, that I should have been better off, but I found it was but going from one butcher to another. There was this difference between them: my former master used to beat me while raging and foaming with passion; Mr. D—— was usually quite calm. He would stand by and give orders for a slave to be cruelly whipped, and assist in the punishment, without moving a muscle of his face" (10).

Female Gothic novelists also represent society as thoroughly corrupt and constantly frightening. In Ann Radcliffe's novels, danger to heroines is omnipresent. If a woman tries to flee from an oppressor, she often finds that there is nowhere to go. Like Mary Prince, when Emily St. Aubert in *The Mysteries of Udolpho* contemplates running away from Montoni, she realizes that "in flying to [her uncle] she could only obtain an exchange of oppressors" (203). Radcliffe's heroines repeatedly discover that every walk they take may lead them into a trap; every building they enter, hoping for a safe home or temporary shelter from a storm, may turn out to be a den of rapists, bandits, and assassins. Near the end of *Udolpho*, Emily tries to laugh away the fears of her female companions by stating ironically, "I perceive . . . that all old mansions are haunted; I am lately come from a place of wonders; but unluckily, since I left it, I have heard almost all of them explained" (491). As soon as the words are out of her mouth, she remembers various unexplained spectacles and secrets, and "shudder[s] at the meaning they seemed to impart" (491). Udolpho may not contain any ghosts or supernatural wonders, but it does house many man-made horrors, including religious grotesquerie, wife abuse, murder, and attempted rape.[5]

Radcliffe and her female readers understood at some level that something was terrifyingly wrong in their culture. However, Radcliffe displaces terror onto a distant place and time. An insight of Alice Miller's helps to account for Radcliffe's exoticism: "A frequent form of resistance [to overly painful truth] is that of temporal and spatial displacement. Thus, for example, it is easier for us to imagine that children were mistreated in previous centuries or are so in distant countries than to recognize the truth about our own country" (*For Your Own Good* 234). This observation illuminates the significance of Jane Austen's place in the female Gothic tradition. In *Northanger Abbey* Austen replaces Radcliffe's exotic sixteenth-century Italian settings with late eighteenth-century English settings that would be familiar to her readers. With characteristic irony Austen domesticates the exotic, only to make the domestic appear alien.

Tania Modleski observes that Jane Austen "began her career not simply burlesquing the Gothic tradition but extracting its core of truth" (21). Evil does not appear as a cosmic mystery in female Gothic but as a human production grounded in men's social position, a position that allows them to pursue, without fear of women's reprisal, their own greed, lust, and ambition. As Alan McKillop notes, "When General Tilney abruptly and rudely sends Catherine home, he gives a pretty good imitation of Montoni in real life, the British domestic subvariety of the Gothic tyrant" (45). General Tilney is a mundane English villain who simply uses the power that English convention and law place in his hands. He is at home in England, a respectable member of the Establishment. He does not kill his wife with physical violence or poison, but he may very well have sent her to an early grave by commonplace husbandly tyranny. He terrifies his children and jeopardizes Catherine's reputation and life by expelling her from his house.

Mary Shelley built on the villains of Radcliffe and Austen by creating a character who, despite (or because of) his good intentions and education, is capable of devising technology that could jeopardize the entire world. In keeping with what M. H. Abrams describes as "the general tendency [of the early 1800s] in diverse degrees and ways, to naturalize the supernatural and to humanize the divine" (68), Mary Shelley replaces the supernatural with the scientific in *Frankenstein*, a move which makes her novel more relevant and more frightening to nineteenth- and twentieth-century readers than tales of the supernatural could be. She represents Victor Frankenstein as an emblem of male irresponsibility and egomaniacal ambition—a prototypical patriarch who is able to create and to destroy but unable to nurture.

Shelley suggests that Frankenstein's inability to recognize the inner life of another human being and to connect genuinely with his own emotional life is the result of his childhood. First, his mother is a model of self-sacrifice who, as Jessica Benjamin describes it, "obliterates herself and her own interests and allows herself to be wholly controlled, [and thus] ceases to become a viable other for him" (39). Second, Frankenstein's narrative suggests that his father was not much involved in his life. Third, Frankenstein consistently idealizes his childhood, claiming that his parents "seemed to draw inexhaustible stores of affection from a very mine of love to bestow them on me. . . . I was their idol and their plaything, and something better—their child, the innocent and helpless creature bestowed on them by heaven. . . . It may be imagined that while during every hour of my infant life I received a lesson of patience, of charity, and of self-control, I was so guided by a silken cord that all seemed but one train of enjoyment to me" (78). Because Frankenstein's parents set no boundaries to his will, he learns to view everyone and everything as his possession. His mother tells him his adopted sister Elizabeth is "a pretty present for my Victor" and he "interpreted her words literally and looked upon Elizabeth as mine—mine to protect, love, and cherish" (80). He also looks on Nature as his possession, desiring to learn her secrets, to plunder her resources for the "benefit" of mankind.[6]

Whether her insights were conscious or subconscious, Mary Shelley powerfully dramatized the results of Victor Frankenstein's lack of ego boundaries and his persistent idealizations of himself and his family. He becomes obsessed with death and begins fantasizing the murder of those he purports to cherish. Eventually his emotional isolation leads him to create the murderer of everyone he "loves." In contrast to his creature, whose violence affirms life insofar as it springs from a desperate need to be connected to other people, Victor is truly necrophilic—pathologically obsessed with corpses, decay, and filth (see Bayer-Berenbaum 134).

In *The Bonds of Love: Psychoanalysis, Feminism, and the Problem of Domination*, Jessica Benjamin describes how personalities like Frankenstein develop: "The child who feels that others are extensions of himself must constantly fear the emptiness and loss of connection that result from his fearful power. Only he exists; the other is effaced, has nothing real to give him. The painful result of success in the battle for omnipotence is that to win is to win nothing: the result is negation, emptiness, isolation" (35). Frankenstein indeed wins nothing in Shelley's novel; before his death, he observes that "like the archangel who aspired to omnipotence, I am chained in an eternal hell" (250).

In *Mathilda* Mary Shelley represents another dysfunctional father who, like Victor Frankenstein, grew up as a wealthy, spoiled child with no ego boundaries. In this autobiographical novella, Shelley explicitly analyzes the incestuous nature of the patriarchal family, which she had thinly disguised in *Frankenstein*. Like Mary Wollstonecraft, Mathilda's mother dies a few days after giving birth. Mathilda's father abandons his newborn daughter to his sister, and then, after sixteen years, returns to claim her. In a pattern similar to William Godwin's treatment of Mary, Mathilda's father alternately lavishes his daughter with attention and coldly neglects her. Tormented by his extreme moods, Mathilda, who "from infancy . . . was deprived of all the testimonies of affection which children generally receive," begs him to share his troubles with her (78). He finally says that he is in love with her and unable to conquer his passion. He revels in the knowledge that he is "all the world" to her; he cannot bear the idea that she might "become the object of another's love . . . or that [she] might love another" (39). After this terrible confession, he commits suicide. Feeling abandoned, monstrous, and guilty of patricide, Mathilda sinks into unmitigated despair.

Shelley wrote *Mathilda* in 1819, but it remained unpublished until 1959. Later female Gothic novelists did not address issues of incest nearly as explicitly as Shelley did. However, authors like the Brontës continued to build on the tradition of Radcliffe, Austen, and Shelley by locating their stories very carefully in historical time and place, to the extent that Charlotte's exposé of the abuse of pupils at Jane Eyre's Lowood, a school very much like the historical Cowan Bridge, caused "a great cry of indignation" and threats of legal proceedings from the friends and patrons of Cowan Bridge (Peters 15).[7] Emily's precise descriptions of Yorkshire (from landscape to language to law) in *Wuthering Heights* and Anne's detailed analysis of alcoholism in *The Tenant of Wildfell Hall* also attest to their courageous recognition that Gothic horror was located in the heart of England and in the homes of respectable people.[8]

In *Wuthering Heights* Emily Brontë suggests that all people, regardless of gender, class, or age, have a propensity for violence and cruelty that is fostered in a patriarchal culture. All her characters are thoroughly infected by what Alice Miller calls "poisonous pedagogy." The insipid, self-deluded Lockwood viciously saws the waif's wrist over the broken windowpane in his dream "till the blood ran down and soaked the bed-clothes" (67). He delights in imagining himself breaking the hearts and crushing the dreams of women. All of the members of the Earnshaw household are initially cruel to Heathcliff, except the father, who is cruel to his family. The pampered Edgar and Isabella are viciously petty, nearly ripping their dog in half the first time Catherine and Heathcliff see them. The young Linton is spineless but tyrannical, while the second Cathy becomes fierce at the Heights. Nelly Dean's maternal protectiveness is always self-interested; as Gilbert and Gubar point out, she aligns herself with the master who pays her and acts "throughout the novel as a censorious agent of patriarchy" (292). She is harshly judgmental of and cruel to Heathcliff and Catherine as well as to the novel's less sympathetic characters, such as the dying Linton. And Joseph, of course, is a grotesquely sadistic religious fanatic.

Slave narratives also represent cruelty as spreading throughout society. Frederick Douglass is particularly insightful about the pervasiveness of the corruption. He points out that his first heartbreak was inflicted by his grandmother, against her will. When he is very small, he lives with many young children in a little cabin where they are cared for by his grandparents. His grandmother is, "at that time, all the world to me"—"a woman of power and spirit. She was marvelously straight in figure, elastic, and muscular," and the young Frederick adores her (*My Bondage* 30, 35). This seemingly powerful woman is forced to bring each of her charges to the master, Colonel Lloyd, as soon as they are old enough to work (seven or eight years old). She sadly brings Douglass on a twelve-mile journey to the main plantation and tells him to go play, and then leaves him without explanation and without saying goodbye. Douglass experiences the anguish of abandonment and betrayal, recalling in his narrative that "I had never been deceived before; and I felt not only grieved at parting—as I supposed forever—with my grandmother, but indignant that a trick had been played upon me in a matter so serious" (36).

Douglass does not blame his grandmother for this betrayal; he holds slaveholders "individually and collectively responsible for all the evils which grow out of the horrid relation. . . . Freedom of choice is the essence of all accountability" (*My Bondage* 119). The clarity of Douglass's social analysis is largely due to his ability to recognize and validate his childhood pain; he insists that "children have their sorrows as well as men and women" (30). He treats his childhood self with respect, observing that "there are thoughtful days in the lives of children— at least there were in mine—when they grapple with all the great, primary subjects of knowledge, and reach, in a moment, conclusions which no subsequent experience can shake. I was just as well aware of the unjust, unnatural and murderous character of slavery, when nine years old, as I am now" (85).

Occasionally, however, Douglass appears either to be confused himself by the dominant notions of childrearing or to be uncertain about how to describe his childhood suffering to an audience unused to crediting children's experiences. Because child abuse was so rampant, Douglass says that he has "nothing cruel or unusual to relate" about his experiences at Colonel Lloyd's plantation, just "an occasional cuff from Aunt Katy, and a regular whipping from old master, such as any heedless and mischievous boy might get from his father" (83). Two pages later, he describes his actual wretchedness: "The cruelty of Aunt Katy, the hunger and cold I suffered, and the terrible reports of wrong and outrage which came to my ear, together with what I almost daily witnessed, led me, when yet but eight or nine years old, to wish I had never been born" (85).

Aunt Katy is one of Douglass's most striking examples of how slavery poisons everyone in society. She is an enslaved woman who is both victim and victimizer. Because of her cooking abilities and industrious personality, she "had a strong hold on old master" (51). Douglass points out, however, that "everybody, in the south, wants the privilege of whipping somebody else" (50). Aunt Katy uses her relative amount of power to tyrannize over other slaves, particularly children. "Ambitious, ill-tempered and cruel," she beats and starves the children around her, including her own offspring. "She was often fiendish in her brutality," observes Douglass. "She pursued her son Phil, one day, in my presence, with a huge butcher knife, and dealt a blow with its edge which left a shocking gash on his arm" (51). Douglass gives many such examples of cruelty to show that the "overshadowing evil" of slavery affects everyone. The whip, both a symbol and a direct instrument of domination, is widely regarded as "all in all" (50).

Slave narratives insist that sadism is inherent to slavery and that slaveholders are responsible for all of the evils the system produces. They depict slave masters and their white sons as similar in many ways to Victor Frankenstein. One cannot say with Jessica Benjamin that slaveholding men "won nothing" in their battles for omnipotence—they could eat sumptuously while their slaves starved, dress elegantly while their slaves went unclothed, and laze about while their slaves died from exhaustion. They also were free to study, to travel, and to choose associates. However, the narratives suggest that the inner existence of slaveholders was indeed filled with the "negation, emptiness and isolation" that Benjamin predicts. Often the sons were subjected to severe physical abuse by their fathers, but they held unchecked power over all other members of the household. Like their fathers, they often viciously abused their power. Yet, like Mary Shelley, the authors of slave narratives show that the men who desired omnipotence made themselves profoundly miserable. Jacobs, for example, describes Dr. Flint as a "vile monster" who is "jealous of his son," jealous of his overseer, jealous of Jacobs's lovers, and constantly angry, contentious, and bitter (27, 41).

If the patriarchal household is a hothouse for vice, the authors of Gothic novels and slave narratives suggest that other social institutions—especially religion and the law—are equally frightening. Frederick Douglass adopted Gothic imagery to vent his anger at southern

Christianity: "The religion of the south is a mere covering for the most horrid crimes,—a justifier of the most appalling barbarity,—a sanctifier of the most hateful frauds,—and a dark shelter under which the darkest, foulest, grossest, and most infernal deeds of slaveholders find the strongest protection. Were I to be again reduced to the chains of slavery, next to that enslavement, I should regard being the slave of a religious master the greatest calamity that could befall me" (*Narrative* 110). More tongue-in-cheek than Douglass, Jacobs observed that "the slaveholders came to the conclusion that it would be well to give the slaves enough of religious instruction to keep them from murdering their masters" (68). Unimpressed, the slaves listened to "sanctimonious" sermons telling them to "be faithful servants" and to obey their masters and mistresses. After receiving such religious instruction, Jacobs and her friends "went home, highly amused," and voiced their opinion of southern religion in songs like "Ole Satan's church is here below" (69, 71).

In keeping with Douglass's tone, Gothic fiction since *The Castle of Otranto* has represented religion, particularly the Catholic church, as the site of all sorts of horrors. Male writers like Lewis and Maturin (a Protestant minister) used their texts to express virulently anti-Catholic and antisemitic passions, whereas female writers launched a broad attack on religious institutions of many kinds. The Gothic novels of Ann Radcliffe and Charlotte Brontë explore the seductive power of the Catholic church's paternalism and depict the church's huge edifices as secretive mazes that could provide cover for incest, rape, torture, and murder. In *Shirley* Brontë severely satirizes Protestant curates, as does Jane Austen in many of her novels and letters.

Like Mary Wollstonecraft, Emily Brontë was skeptical of all religious systems. In "No Coward Soul Is Mine," she argues:

> Vain are the thousand creeds
> That move men's hearts, unutterably vain,
> Worthless as withered weeds
> Or idlest froth amid the boundless main.

For Brontë, as for American slaves and Gothic heroines, the challenge is to construct a life-sustaining belief system that will help one to escape from the labyrinths of the patriarchal family, religion, and law.

DENIAL OF KNOWLEDGE

Arguing against Max Weber's idea that "the decisive means for politics is violence," Eugene Genovese points to the central function of ideology, particularly "the theoretical and moral foundations of the legal order," in the maintenance of the power structure (25). He argues that "no class in the modern Western world could rule for long without some ability to present itself as the guardian of the interests and sentiments of those being ruled" (25). John Sekora extends Genovese's analysis by showing that the slaveholders' attempts to control slaves' views of the world extended far beyond their use of the legal system as a hegemonic force: "Slaveowners possessed the increasingly elaborate state codes controlling the labor and physical being of slaves. Yet they sought more—even the words, the very language of their slaves. . . . By seeking to control slave language, masters sought to exact slave complicity in their own subjugation" ("Black Message" 485). Because of the centrality of language, Sekora continues, "slavery [is] very much a literary matter. Slavery and the language of slavery are virtually coextensive" (485).

John Stuart Mill and Harriet Jacobs were well aware of the phenomenon observed by Genovese and Sekora. Like many nineteenth-century feminist-abolitionists, Mill and Jacobs emphasized in their writings that the men who dominated women and enslaved Africans attempted to colonize the minds as well as the bodies of their subjects. Mill observes in *The Subjection of Women* that "all men, except the most brutish, desire to have, in the woman most nearly connected with them, not a forced slave but a willing one, not a slave merely, but a favorite. They have therefore put everything in practice to enslave their minds." In *Incidents* Jacobs shows that Dr. Flint attempted to colonize and subjugate her mind: "he peopled my young mind with unclean images" (27). Because knowledge is power, slaveholders denied knowledge to slaves. Jacobs was more fortunate than many American slaves because she "lived in a town where all the inhabitants knew each other" (35). Even when slavery was the common way of life and white male dominance appeared absolute, women found power in knowledge.

Regarding their treatment of slaves, white southern men had nothing to fear from the law, for two reasons: the Dred Scott decision of 1857 proclaimed that blacks "had no rights which the white man was bound to respect," and, to emphasize this fact, slaves were not allowed to testify against whites in court. Nonetheless, slaveholders frantically shrouded their actions in secrecy; for a slave to tell the truth about the activities of a slaveholder was punishable by death. "Free" blacks in the North were also routinely denied the right to *know*—the right to education and to speech. Significantly, the "first American woman on record to present a public lecture" was an African American who attacked the dominant culture's repression of knowledge (Yellin, *Women and Sisters* 46). In Boston on September 21, 1832, Maria W. Stewart declared that "there are no chains as galling as the chains of ignorance— no fetters so binding as those that bind the soul, and exclude it from the vast fund of useful and scientific knowledge" (qtd. in Yellin 46).

In *The Contested Castle*, Kate Ferguson Ellis shows that eighteenth- and nineteenth-century Gothic novelists, reacting against the conventions that demanded innocence of women, consistently dramatized the danger of innocence to the health of their characters. Time and again, Gothic novels show that "innocence that is an ignorance of evil, however defined, [is] by its very definition defenseless against what it did not know" (15). In Gothic novels written by men, such as *The Castle of Otranto*, *The Monk*, and *Melmoth the Wanderer*, innocent heroines are routinely raped, tortured, and killed. In Gothic novels written by women, innocent heroines are usually guided by the authors into an understanding of human evil, a knowledge that in many cases empowers them to survive and to escape from the severe forms of victimization that male Gothic novelists delight in depicting.

In a revealing moment in *The Mysteries of Udolpho*, Emily St. Aubert looks at Montoni and exclaims to herself, "O could I know . . . what passes in that mind; could I know the thoughts, that are known there, I should no longer be condemned to this torturing suspense!" (243). The central mystery of female Gothic is the bizarre behavior of men whose actions appear malicious and whose motives are veiled. Forced into an "innocence" that mystifies power relations, untrained to read men, heroines like Emily "could scarcely have imagined, that passions so fierce and so various, as those which Montoni exhibited, could have been concentrated in one individual; yet what more surprised her, was, that, on great occasions, he could bend these passions, wild as they were, to the cause of his interest" (296). Women cannot escape the *experience* of evil, but they are denied the *knowledge* of it. Uninformed but suspicious about Montoni, "Emily observed [his fierce countenance] with deep interest, and not without some degree of awe, when she considered that she was entirely in his power" (192).

Emily's immersion in "innocence" is enforced originally by her "good" father, St. Aubert. She begins life in an idyllic home with parents who are too good for this world. Her mother catches fever while nursing her father and dies in the first chapter. Shortly thereafter, St. Aubert, on his deathbed, asks Emily to burn some of his papers without reading them, thus simultaneously piquing her curiosity and refusing to satisfy it. Radcliffe makes it clear in the novel that the ignorance that St. Aubert's secrecy forces upon Emily jeopardizes her life.

Emily's experiences in *Udolpho* show that if heroines are to survive, they must learn to recognize evil when they encounter it. Montoni intends to profit from Emily in two ways: by selling her into marriage and by compelling her to sign over her inheritance to him. He advises her "to spare himself and her the trouble of useless contest, in an affair, where his will was justice, and where she would find it law" (380). Like Madame Montoni, Emily learns that people with power are capable of great injustice, and this knowledge "roused all the latent powers of her fortitude into action; and the property, which she would willingly have resigned to secure the peace of her aunt, she resolved, that no common sufferings of her own should ever compel her to give to Montoni" (379). Understanding Montoni demystifies his power. After Emily sees Montoni for the villain that he is, "his power did not appear so terrible to her imagination, as it was wont to do; a sacred pride was in her heart, that taught it to swell against the pressure of injustice. . . . For the first time, she felt the full extent of her own superiority to Montoni, and despised the authority, which, till now, she had only feared" (381–82). Thus Radcliffe shows how enforced "innocence" disempowers women, whereas knowledge of evil enables resistance. The narrator of *The Romance of the Forest* states that "confidence in the sincerity and goodness of others was [the heroine's] weakness" (47). Although this statement may appear to be a conventional compliment to the heroine's virtue, in fact the novel underscores the dangers of trusting people too readily. Ignorance of the existence of evil in the world mystifies and strengthens tyranny, whereas recognition of injustice enables people to resist it, at least internally.

In *The Mysteries of Udolpho* Emily's innocence is contrasted to Madame Cheron-Montoni's cynicism. The latter, although she is worldly wise and experienced in society, is actually as unprepared as Emily to be adequately suspicious (or "righteously paranoid") of male behavior.[9] Cheron's tendency to suspect people of wrongdoing is not based on a genuine understanding of evil. She quickly and falsely accuses Emily of multiple indiscretions but is blind to Montoni's self-

interest. Her "worldly wisdom" consists mainly in her habit of irratio-
nally condemning those people over whom she has power while overlooking early danger signs in relationships with those people who have
power over her. Her marriage to Montoni is only the most catastrophic
mistake in her long history of misjudgments.

Jane Austen understood the significance of Radcliffe's analysis of
the dangers of innocence. In *Northanger Abbey*, Catherine Morland is
able to suspect General Tilney of villainy because she has read numerous Gothic novels. She has been particularly enlightened by reading
The Mysteries of Udolpho. Henry Tilney may mock her reading; nonetheless, as Kate Ellis notes, "Catherine's only preparation for the general's reckless endangerment of her person comes from the pages of
Radcliffe" (5). Austen's narrator states that Catherine has learned by
the end of the novel that her suspicions of General Tilney were not
far off the mark: "Catherine, at any rate, heard enough to feel, that
in suspecting General Tilney of either murdering or shutting up his
wife, she had scarcely sinned against his character, or magnified his
cruelty" (243). However, *Northanger Abbey* also suggests that because
books like *The Mysteries of Udolpho* place villains in exotic distant lands,
they mystify evil almost as much as they illuminate it. Austen teaches
her heroine that evil is mundane and banal more often than it is dramatic and exotic. In the final analysis, Catherine's Gothic education
does not *adequately* prepare her to deal with men like General Tilney
and John Thorpe, but reading Gothic novels at least forewarns her
that all is not right with the world.

In *Jane Eyre* Charlotte Brontë examines a variety of techniques
men use to deny knowledge to women. Like most masculinist critics
of women's texts, Rochester attempts to dismiss Jane's recounting of
her encounter with Bertha by labeling Bertha simply a "creature of
[Jane's] over-stimulated brain" (312). When Jane produces the torn
veil as physical evidence that her story is true, Rochester again dis-
counts her text by fabricating a "rational" explanation. He knows that
his power to act as he wishes is based largely on secrecy and lies. He
has confessed to Jane a few sexual "indiscretions," a few torrid affairs, representing himself as a victim of the cold world as well as a
sexual conqueror. He cannot, however, bring himself to mention the
major story: the hideous reality of his relationship with Bertha. Linda
Kauffman argues insightfully that Bertha is "a mute symbol of how
disobedient women are silenced and driven mad under the supervi-
sion of so-called rational men" (188). Bertha is a victim not simply of

Rochester but of the social system that allows men to exchange women as objects of trade. Rochester's father and brother, as well as Bertha's male relatives, all hope to benefit from this marriage transaction, one which takes place secretly between men in the West Indies.

Rochester's courtship of Jane is a series of disguises. He adopts a variety of emotional postures in repeated attempts to manipulate Jane's emotions and behavior. He pretends indifference or passion as it suits him; he "feigns courtship" of Blanche Ingram in order "to render [Jane] madly in love" (*Jane Eyre* 291); he pretends to be a gypsy fortune-teller in order to elicit a confession of love from Jane. Preferring "to make Jane doubt her own sanity, rather than reveal his duplicity," he "comes close to making Jane as mad as Bertha is" (Kauffman 191).

Brontë shows that for a woman to be "reasonable" means for her to accept a man's reading of a situation. Rochester is enraged when Jane refuses to accept his explanation that his marriage to Bertha is not real and that a union with Jane would be sanctified by their personal pledges of fidelity. Jane, however, remembers the fate of his previous mistresses, for whom he now has no feelings but contempt. She understands that social mores and economic realities would place all the risks of an illicit liaison on her side. When she refuses to yield to Rochester's "logic," he exclaims, "What a distortion in your judgement, what a perversity in your ideas, is proved by your conduct! Is it better to drive a fellow-creature to despair than to transgress a mere human law, no man being injured by the breach?" (343). Jane is caught here between the competing claims of male logic, male desire, male laws, and male-dominated economic reality. She feels confused and trapped: "While he spoke my very conscience and reason turned traitors against me, and charged me with crime in resisting him. They spoke almost as loud as Feeling: and that clamoured wildly. 'Oh, comply!' it said. 'Think of his misery; think of his danger; look at his state when left alone; remember his headlong nature; consider the recklessness following on despair—soothe him; save him; love him; tell him you love him and will be his. Who in the world cares for *you*? or who will be injured by what you do?'" (344). By using the words "him" and "his" eleven times in this short passage, Brontë emphasizes the force of the ideological assault on Jane's self-esteem. Jane has been trained to believe that women were created to serve men, not to consider their own needs and desires.

This is a crucial moment in Jane's life, like the crisis that faces many

Gothic heroines who are not only socially disempowered but also internally subjected to male-prescribed reason and emotion. Furthermore, what Daniel Cottom observes about Jane Austen's novels fits a general pattern in female Gothic: "At any moment women . . . may be judged not to know their own meaning. Their opinion of what they think, of what they know, and even of what they feel may be overruled by the opinion of men" (75). From the moment when Jane first encounters Rochester and he fails to mention his identity as her employer until the moment when she runs away from Thornfield, Rochester gains and maintains power through secrecy, silence, and misinformation. To survive, Jane must not only unmask his deceptions, but also withstand the force of the entire cultural system that validates Rochester's point of view.

In a similar but more sinister manner, Dr. Flint's attempts to seduce Linda Brent involve an endless process of posturing and manipulation. He poses as a fatherly protector, an impassioned lover, an omnipotent master, a concerned friend, a born-again Christian—all disguises adopted to mystify the reality that he is a sadistic petty tyrant. A significant difference between Linda Brent and Jane Eyre, however, is that Linda always knows that Flint is lying. As Jacobs represents her story, Linda sees through all of Flint's schemes. The material realities of slavery did not permit many romantic mystifications for the slaves, although the masters tried constantly to generate a false consciousness for both themselves and the people they oppressed.

Unlike Linda Brent, Mary Shelley's Mathilda is painfully confused by the men who mistreat her. She finds her father's mind "diseased yet incomprehensible" (20). Idealizing men, she berates herself for negative feelings. Her father blames her for her mother's death and for his incestuous desire, accusing her of being "the sole, the agonizing cause of all I suffer, of all I must suffer untill [sic] I die. Now, beware! Be silent! Do not urge me to your destruction" (29). Like many victims of incest, Mathilda internalizes her father's blame: "I believed myself to be polluted by the unnatural love I had inspired, and that I was a creature cursed and set apart by nature" (71). Like Frankenstein's creature, Mathilda sees herself as a "monster with whom none might mingle in converse and love" (71).

When Mathilda forms a brief friendship with a poet named Woodville (a representation of Percy Shelley), she idealizes him as "the most gentle and sympathizing creature that existed" (64). She laments the fact that she sometimes gets "angry, very angry" at him, concluding that "I had become captious and unreasonable: my temper was utterly spoilt" (64). At one point, however, Mary's text erupts in a powerful, clearly autobiographical expression of her resentment against Percy, the "great" poet: "I am, I thought, a tragedy; a character he comes to see act: now and then he gives me my cue that I may make a speech more to his purpose: perhaps he is already planning a poem in which I am to figure. I am a farce and play to him, but to me this is all dreary reality: he takes all the profit and I bear all the burthen" (65). In the end, Mathilda understands that because "I never dared give words to my dark tale, I was impressed more strongly with the withering fear that I was in truth a marked creature, a pariah, only fit for death" (72). Her one act of self-affirmation is to write her story before dying.

Female Gothic novelists often were afraid of their rage, and authors of slave narratives often were forced to censor expressions of their rage and desire for revenge. Nonetheless, both genres seethe with anger against the would-be playwrights who attempted to dictate the scripts of their lives—mandating not only what they could say but also what they could know.

IN *The History of Sexuality*, Foucault analyzes some of the ways in which silences and myths about silence can simultaneously support and undermine the power structure. "Discourse," he observes, "transmits and produces power; it reinforces it, but also undermines and exposes it, renders it fragile and makes it possible to thwart it. In like manner, silence and secrecy are a shelter for power, anchoring its prohibitions; but they also loosen its holds and provide for relatively obscure areas of tolerance" (101). Although human beings are severely damaged by lies, secrets, and silence, in some cases oppressed people can use the gaps and contradictions in the dominant discourse as a base or cover for resistance.

It is important, however, to remember that millions of people have been lost forever in the labyrinths of terror described by slave narrators and female Gothic novelists. In *Beloved* Toni Morrison eulogizes the millions of enslaved Africans who are "disremembered and unaccounted for," the "dearly beloved" whose stories have been irrecoverably lost. Morrison's ghostly character, Beloved, is a poignant reminder that millions of silences will never be broken: "Everybody knew what she was called, but nobody knew her name. Disremembered and unaccounted for, she cannot be lost because no one is looking for her, and even if they were, how can they call her if they don't know her name? Although she has claim, she is not claimed. . . . It was not a story to pass on" (274). Every text written by a woman between 1790 and 1865 was to some extent an act of resistance and in some way a triumph against the dominant culture. While we celebrate the successes of these women, we must also try to acknowledge the significance of the stories that were not passed on, the part of our history that we have not claimed and that we do not know how to claim.

3
SISTERHOOD
IN
SLAVERY?

I once saw two beautiful children playing together. One was a fair white child;
the other was her slave, and also her sister. When I saw them embracing each
other, and heard their joyous laughter, I turned sadly away from the lovely sight.

Harriet Jacobs

IN ANTEBELLUM AMERICA the terms "brother" and "sister" gained a
special force among African Americans, many of whom were violently separated from their biological siblings. In African-American
usage to this day, "brother" and "sister" are honorific titles that mark
a shared humanity, a sense of collectivity. Perhaps these terms derive
their continuing force in African-American speech because of the historical situation of that particular community: African Americans do
indeed share a particular kind of kinship, the experience of life behind the veil, in W. E. B. Du Bois's terms, or a condition of invisibility,
in Ralph Ellison's terms. At the same time, "brother" and "sister"
are gender-bound terms that mark a primary division that continues
within the black as well as the white world.

As an ideal to strive towards, "sisterhood" can be a powerful concept. Unfortunately, many feminists in the current wave of the women's
movement have used the term as if it described a *reality* of women's
universal solidarity: "Sisterhood *is* powerful." As a consequence, many
of us have ignored and perpetuated our own heterosexism, racism,
and classism.

Reacting against the feminists who ignored differences among
women while projecting an ideal of sisterhood, many working-class
feminists, lesbians, and women of color have argued that the term
"sisterhood" misleads by obscuring historical realities and so prevents
women from confronting divisive problems. Bell Hooks points out
that "all too frequently in the women's movement it was assumed . . .
that identifying oneself as oppressed freed one from being an oppressor. To a very grave extent such thinking prevented white feminists

from understanding and overcoming their own sexist-racist attitudes toward black women. They could pay lip service to the idea of sisterhood and solidarity between women but at the same time dismiss black women" (8–9). The tendency of white middle-class women to idealize sisterhood while oppressing their black sisters has a long history in the United States. Minrose Gwin, in *Black and White Women of the Old South* (1985), shows that the novels of the abolitionist Harriet Beecher Stowe (*Uncle Tom's Cabin*, 1851) and the pro-slavery advocate Mary H. Eastman (*Aunt Phillis's Cabin*, 1852) "contain an almost identical subtext: the power of cross-racial female bonds in opposition to the male sphere" (43). At the same time, both novels represent black women in stereotypical, racist ways, and both novelists often mistreated black women in their personal lives.

In *Women and Sisters: The Antislavery Feminists in American Culture* (1989), Jean Fagan Yellin shows how powerful sisterhood can be when women join forces to fight against oppression. In the antebellum period, white and black feminist-abolitionists used an emblem depicting a black woman, "half nude, chained, kneeling in supplication," as the unofficial symbol of their struggle (3). Above the picture was the motto, "Am I Not a Woman and a Sister?" Abolitionist women embroidered this emblem on thousands of articles, used it to illustrate books, printed it on stationery, stamped it on metal tokens, and reproduced it in newspapers and periodicals. By 1836 white and black women had formed over sixty American antislavery societies, and between 1835 and 1865 "hundreds of thousands of American women petitioned federal, state, and local governments on the slaves' behalf" (39). Abolitionist-feminism was plagued by racism, classism, and insidious patriarchal values, but nonetheless Angelina Grimké was right when she declared that "We Abolition Women are turning the world upside-down!" (42). Yellin's work powerfully exhorts us not to forget the significance of what black and white feminist-abolitionists accomplished in the mid-nineteenth century—not to participate in the dominant culture's appropriation and silencing of "the antislavery feminists' oppositional discourse" (xvii).

Although sisterhood can be powerful, it can also be horrific. In *Within the Plantation Household: Black and White Women of the Old South* (1988), Elizabeth Fox-Genovese uses the term "sisterhood" not to designate solidarity but rather to describe the physical proximity of white and black women in southern households. She shows that although many slaveholding women were elitist, racist, and even vicious, they shared with slave women "a world of physical and emotional intimacy" (35). In many instances, slaveholders and slaves were *biological* siblings. The phrase "my family, white and black" was commonplace among southern whites, and it fittingly summarizes the problematic condition of slaveholder's paternalistic ideology. On the one hand, the phrase suggests intimacy. On the other, it indicates the paterfamilias's sense of ownership of all members of the household and sustains the cultural distinction between white and black. The ominous aspect of the phrase is clear when one considers that the paterfamilias was often— by means of systematic sexual exploitation—the biological father of his family, white and black. Ultimately, then, southern paternalism literally subverted its own racism: by fathering children of more than one "race," the paterfamilias inadvertently and unconsciously called race itself into question.[1] Such fathers typically enslaved or sold their own "black" children. (Jacobs observes that Dr. Flint sold eleven of his children and their mothers.) In short, members of the southern "family" were victims of "the grotesque intimacies that arose from the perverse paternalism of the South's peculiar institution" (Andrews, Introduction xix).

The "grotesque intimacies" of the southern household infected every aspect of life. One of the most perverse practices was the use of slave women to nurse the white children who would grow up to be their owners and masters. Often slave women were forced to deprive their own children of much-needed nourishment in order to feed the master class. Jacobs, for example, observes that her "mother had been weaned at three months old, that the babe of the mistress might obtain sufficient food" (7). Through this outrageous practice, white infants literally sucked health and strength out of the bodies of adult slaves at the emotional and physical expense of black infants.

In patriarchal cultures, of which the antebellum South is an extreme example, families are perhaps as often the locus of hatred, violence, and destruction as of love, nurture, and support. Like spouses, brothers, parents, and children, sisters share a profound but not necessarily positive relationship. In the patriarchal family, sisters share the condition of being subjected to the father's law, and this joint subjection sometimes leads to feelings of solidarity. However, sisters are just as likely to betray each other as to support each other, especially when one sister is culturally empowered over the other because of her race and class.

When we focus attention on relations between women rather than on relations between fathers and daughters, we can see how women have been not only subjects of slavery but also agents of history. That is to say, women have worked both as mediators of the patriarchal order (participants in their own subjugation and the subjugation of other women) and as initiators of historical change—liberators of themselves and other women.

RACE AND CLASS DIVISIONS

In her unfinished Gothic novel *The Wrongs of Woman*, Mary Wollstonecraft sets out to demonstrate that "the wrongs of different classes of women [are] equally oppressive, though, from the difference of education, necessarily various" (74). A radical cultural critic, Wollstonecraft describes in realistic terms the brutal economic violence of patriarchal capitalism against all women. Particularly noteworthy is her sensitive portrayal of the gradual degradation of Jemima, a working-class woman who has been subjected to slave labor, rape, and prostitution. Although the fragmented novel devotes more space to the middle-class heroine Maria than to Jemima, Wollstonecraft's purpose is to show that women's only hope for success in their fight against patriarchal domination lies in their ability to unite across class lines. Maria, imprisoned in an insane asylum by her husband, escapes from her prison with the aid of Jemima, who is equally imprisoned by her position as a guard in the asylum.

Ann Radcliffe was writing at the same time as Wollstonecraft, but her work lacks Wollstonecraft's political consciousness. Radcliffe was more interested in locating her writing in a literary tradition than in explicitly analyzing the political realities of her day. Like Shakespeare, she often depicts working-class characters as comically affectionate, loyal, and unintelligent. However, her use of working-class characters as comic foils to the protagonists is riddled with interesting contradictions. Annette, Emily's maid in *The Mysteries of Udolpho*, is a stereotypical chatterbox with whom Emily often loses patience. Annette's predicaments, however, often parallel Emily's in ways that disturb rather than amuse Emily. On several occasions, Emily's laughter at Annette turns into alarm as she recognizes the parallels between them. Like Emily, Annette is imprisoned, tormented, and separated from the man she loves. At the end of their mutual ordeals, Emily provides money for Annette's marriage and employs Annette and her husband as the housekeeper and steward on a "magnificent" estate (672).

Like Austen's heroines and heroes, Emily usually reveals a proper aristocratic sensitivity to the sufferings of working-class characters; she is furious, for example, when her uncle turns out the aged, lame, family servant, Theresa, "without any provision" (592). Emily's sentiments never lead her to any action more radical than the paternalistic determination to treat her servants well by paying them better than average and providing for their retirement; one of her first actions after she finally manages to get back to her home is to make sure Theresa is comfortably provided for. Nonetheless, Radcliffe's novels suggest tentatively what Wollstonecraft declares emphatically: "The wrongs of different classes of women [are] equally oppressive."

In *Incidents in the Life of a Slave Girl*, Harriet Jacobs dramatically represents the peculiar sisterhood of black and white women in the Old South. Her sensitive social analysis illuminates the ways the southern patriarchal order intertwined race, gender, and class oppressions. Although her central concern is to expose the sufferings of enslaved women, she also provides many examples of the wretchedness of white wives who have "romantic notions" of the happiness they will find in marriage, only to learn that marriage deprives them of their fortunes and their power over their own lives and that their husbands will father and sell "children of every shade of complexion" (36).

Jacobs focuses her analysis of the situation of white women on Mrs. Flint, a miserable woman who fights daily with her abusive, lecherous husband. Jacobs often speaks of the pity she feels for Mrs. Flint, while Mrs. Flint is unable to feel pity for anyone but herself: "She felt that her marriage vows were desecrated, her dignity insulted; but she had no compassion for the poor victim of her husband's perfidy. She pitied herself as a martyr; but she was incapable of feeling for the condition of shame and misery in which her unfortunate, helpless slave was placed" (33). Many unhappy white women like Mrs. Flint saw themselves as martyrs and refused to recognize the humanity of slaves, preferring to abuse their power over their black sisters. However, Kate Drumgoold recalled in 1898 that her unhappy mistress in Virginia turned to her slaves for solace. A kind woman who detested slavery, this mistress "always said that we [the slaves] were all that she had on earth to love; and she did love me to the last" (4). White women could not escape some degree of victimization in the Old South, but they could choose whether to ally themselves with the oppressors or the oppressed.

In her struggle for freedom, Jacobs is aided by countless enslaved women and men and by northern abolitionists. Occasionally, a white southern woman also fights against the social system by aiding slaves in their acts of resistance. At one crucial moment in Jacobs's story, an unnamed white woman from a prestigious slaveholding family risks ruining herself and her family by concealing Jacobs in her house for several weeks.

Jacobs's narrative rarely romanticizes the lives of southern whites. In fact, Jacobs usually describes the complexities of white women's lives with profound insight and clarity, balancing her compassionate reading of white women's victimization with an honest critique of their cruelty. Once in a while, however, Jacobs slips into an idealization of the lives of the women who had much more power and material comfort in their lives than she did. For example, in one significant passage she describes seeing "two beautiful children playing together. One was a fair white child; the other was her slave, and also her sister. When I saw them embracing each other, and heard their joyous laughter, I turned sadly away from the lovely sight. I foresaw the inevitable blight that would fall on the little slave's heart. I knew how soon her laughter would be changed to sighs. The fair child grew up to be a still fairer woman. From childhood to womanhood her pathway was blooming with flowers, and overarched by a sunny sky" (29). The relationship between these two sisters assumes symbolic significance for Jacobs: the girls are biologically and emotionally connected, but a racist-sexist slave culture divides them into representatives of the old dichotomy of angel and whore. From the perspective of the culturally designated whore, the position of the angel in the house may seem enviable indeed: her life appears filled with flowers, sunshine, and happiness.

Ultimately, however, Jacobs's narrative reveals that the angel in the southern patriarch's house is wretched and pitiable. In *Their Eyes Were Watching God* Zora Neale Hurston extends Jacobs's analysis of the dangers of idealizing white women's position in society. Hurston describes Nanny, a former slave who has been emotionally devastated by years of sexual violence, economic exploitation, and psychological abuse. She wants nothing more for her granddaughter Janie than the "protection" and economic security of marriage to a wealthy man (30). Janie spends more than twenty years of her life learning how deadening it is to live with a man who believes that "a pretty doll-baby lak you is made to sit on de front porch and rock and fan yo'self and eat p'taters dat other folk plant just special for you" (49). Janie never suffers the way Nanny suffered, but she dies internally while she is sitting on a pedestal, acting the part of the angel in the house. In the end Hurston suggests that women need to liberate themselves entirely from the angel-whore dichotomy in order to find a life of their own.

Like Harriet Jacobs, Mary Prince insightfully analyzes how black and white women often shared a common bondage as well as the ways in which white women often tyrannized black women. In "The History of Mary Prince, A West Indian Slave" (1831), Prince represents her first master as "a very harsh, selfish man" who terrorized his wife as well as his slaves. Everyone was relieved when he was away from home. Prince emphasizes that she and all of the other slaves "loved and pitied" their abused mistress, who was "a kind-hearted good woman" (1). Years later, Prince jeopardizes her own health to come to the aid of the white daughter of another cruel master, a man who "often got drunk, and then he would get in a fury with his daughter, and beat her till she was not fit to be seen" (13). On one particularly dreadful occasion the man almost kills his daughter; Prince saves the daughter's life by interposing her own body: "I strove with all my strength to get her away from him; for she was all black and blue with bruises. . . . He turned round and began to lick me" (13). A woman of remarkable compassion and courage, Prince risks her life protecting this white woman. Later, she risks her life by *accepting* aid from a group of white women who have organized classes to teach slaves to read.

However, Prince does not idealize white women. Her account of her first kindly mistress and the "Moravian ladies" who taught her to read is balanced by her account of a different mistress. This woman is also a teacher; she instructs Prince in how "to do all sort of household work." In addition, Prince notes, "she taught me (how can I ever forget it!) . . . the exact difference between the smart of the rope, the cart-whip, and the cow-skin, when applied to my naked body by her own cruel hand. And there was scarcely any punishment more dreadful than the blows I received on my face and head from her hard heavy fist. She was a fearful woman, and a savage mistress to her slaves" (6). This savage mistress and her even more savage husband torture and kill many of Prince's fellow slaves. Prince consistently represents masters as cruel and abusive in every way imaginable, whereas mistresses are represented as a complex mixture of victim and victimizer.

Louisa Picquet's narrative attests to a similar mixture of cruelty and friendship between white and black women. Picquet begins her story by relating how her fifteen-year-old mother was sold down the river because the baby Louisa looked too similar to the mistress's own baby. Like many white southern women, Madame Randolph responded to her husband's sexual exploitation of slaves by punishing the slave woman.[2] However, Picquet also relates that when she, like her mother, was subjected to sexual assaults, some white women attempted to rescue her. She is "a little girl, not fourteen years old" when her master, Mr. Cook, attempts to trap her alone in his room to rape her. Two white sisters, Mrs. Bachelor and Mrs. Simpson, protect her for several days by inventing excuses so that Picquet will never be alone with Cook. Eventually, however, the women are unable to provide protection. Picquet is Cook's property, and if he believes she has discussed his intentions with other people, he may kill her. Picquet observes that Mrs. Bachelor "was the best friend I had; but she could not interfere no more, because if she did he'd know that I told her. Then she said she had no patience with him—he was the meanest man she ever saw. She abused him then a great deal, before her sister and before me" (Mattison 14). Finally, Mrs. Bachelor advises Picquet to avoid Cook as much as possible; she does not know how to offer more substantial support. In cases such as this, the system of slavery constricted the ability of well-intentioned white women to befriend black women.

Charlotte Brontë's "madwoman in the attic" has become for twentieth-century feminists a powerful and controversial symbol of the condition of women. In 1966 Jean Rhys called attention to Brontë's problematic representation of a madwoman of mixed race by attempting to tell the story from Bertha Mason's perspective in *Wide Sargasso Sea*. However, in the 1860s Harriet Jacobs had already written, from her own perspective, a story about a black "madwoman" in the attic. If Jacobs, who represented herself (Linda Brent) as a romantic heroine, had read *Jane Eyre*, she probably identified with Jane as much as with Bertha. It is possible that Jacobs was familiar with Brontë's story; at least one slave mother in the 1860s named her daughter Jane Eyre, a sign that the novel was known to some slaves.[3] In any case, in *Incidents in the Life of a Slave Girl* Jacobs represents relations between women in ways that both complement and challenge Brontë's representation.

In a famous passage in *Jane Eyre*, Charlotte Brontë writes:

> It is in vain to say human beings ought to be satisfied with tranquillity: they must have action; and they will make it if they cannot find it. Millions are condemned to a stiller doom than mine, and millions are in silent revolt against their lot. Nobody knows how many rebellions besides political rebellions ferment in the masses of life which people earth. Women are supposed to be very calm generally: but women feel just as men feel; they need exercise for their faculties and a field for their efforts as much as their brothers do; they suffer from too rigid

a restraint, too absolute a stagnation, precisely as men would suffer; and it is narrow-minded in their more privileged fellow-creatures to say that they ought to confine themselves to making puddings and knitting stockings, to playing on the piano and embroidering bags. It is thoughtless to condemn them, or laugh at them, if they seek to do more than custom has pronounced necessary for their sex.

When thus alone, I not infrequently heard Grace Poole's [Bertha Mason's] laugh. (141)

"That is an awkward break," wrote Virginia Woolf in 1929. "It is upsetting to come upon Grace Poole all of a sudden" (72). Woolf continued her critique of *Jane Eyre* by accusing Brontë of allowing "the fact of her sex" to "interfere with [her] integrity. . . . She left her story, to which her entire devotion was due, to attend to some personal grievance" (76).

Woolf's harsh comments about Brontë have prompted not only eighty years of feminist debate about the desirability of women writers expressing anger, but also a plethora of feminist readings of the passage that troubled Woolf. Adrienne Rich reads the passage as "Charlotte Brontë's feminist manifesto" ("Jane Eyre" 97). Gilbert and Gubar cite the abrupt transition from Jane's anger to Bertha Mason's laugh as evidence that Bertha functions as Jane's double, her "secret self" (168).

Cora Kaplan has analyzed the complexities in the above passage more thoroughly than previous critics. She argues that the passage is "a significant moment of incoherence, where the congruence between the subordination of women and the radical view of class oppression becomes, for a few sentences, irresistible" (173). In Kaplan's view, Brontë's moment of radical insight ends with Bertha's laugh because Jane views Bertha not as an ally against patriarchal oppression but as "a threat to all that Jane had desired and demanded in her rooftop reverie" (173–74). Kaplan argues that, for Jane, Bertha "and her noises become the condensed and displaced site of unreason and anarchy as it is metonymically figured through dangerous femininity in all its class, race and cultural projections. Bertha must be killed off, narratively speaking, so that a moral, Protestant femininity, licensed sexuality and a qualified, socialized feminism may survive" (174). However, continues Kaplan, "the text cannot close off or recuperate that moment of radical association between political rebellion and gender rebellion" (174).

I would argue that *Jane Eyre* also cannot close off the possibility of sisterhood between the white middle-class English heroine and the mixed-race declassé foreign madwoman in the attic. Jane is fright-

ened of Bertha partly because she recognizes the fragility of the distinctions between them. She understands that what Bertha suffers,
she also could suffer. Jane's discovery of Rochester's relationship to
Bertha unmasks the horrific possibilities of women's dependency in
a male-dominated society. If Jane were to elope with Rochester, she
could easily become like Bertha: a social alien deprived of every financial and intellectual resource. Bertha's fate is Jane's worst nightmare
come true.[4]

Brontë dramatizes the connections between Bertha and Jane near
the middle of the novel, when Jane awakens one night from a nightmare about falling to her death in the ruins of Thornfield Hall (a
prefiguration of Bertha's final fate). Upon awaking, Jane discovers
"a woman, tall and large, with thick and dark hair" trying on Jane's
wedding veil. Jane sees the reflection in a dark mirror of a "fearful,"
"ghastly," "discoloured," "savage" woman who tears the veil "in two
parts, and flinging both on the floor, trampled on them" (311). This ap-
parition, who is Bertha, moves with a candle to Jane's bedside, where,
Jane says, "the fiery eyes glared upon me—she thrust up her candle
close to my face, and extinguished it under my eyes. I was aware of
her lurid visage flamed over mine, and I lost consciousness" (311–12).

A nocturnal encounter in *Incidents in the Life of a Slave Girl* is strikingly similar to this scene. When the young Jacobs attempts to escape
from the sexual designs of her master, she has to contend with the
jealousy of her mistress, Mrs. Flint. Because Mrs. Flint is unable to
attack her husband directly, she vents her rage on Jacobs. Mrs. Flint
requires Jacobs to sleep "in a room adjoining her own," a require-
ment for which Jacobs is ironically grateful because her proximity to
Mrs. Flint offers some protection against Dr. Flint. During these nights
Jacobs found herself to be

> an object of [Mrs. Flint's] especial care, though not of her especial com-
> fort, for she spent many a sleepless night to watch over me. Sometimes I
> woke up, and found her bending over me. At other times she whispered
> in my ear, as though it was her husband who was speaking to me, and
> listened to hear what I would answer. If she startled me, on such occa-
> sions, she would glide stealthily away. . . . At last, I began to fear for my
> life. It had been often threatened; and you can imagine, better than I
> can describe, what an unpleasant sensation it must produce to wake up
> in the dead of night and find a jealous woman bending over you. (34)

In this passage, as in the passage from *Jane Eyre*, a white woman and
a woman of color are involved in a frightening web of interaction.

The roles of wife and intended "mistress" have been reversed, but in both cases the white woman (whether heroine or villain) is afraid of the woman of color, despite the fact that the white woman herself holds the balance of power. At the same time, the relation between the women is intimate; the boundaries between self and other become remarkably fluid.[5]

In both scenes, the contact between the women briefly establishes a grotesque but useful solidarity against patriarchal advances. Jane may be terrified of Bertha, but she runs away from Rochester. Bertha may resent Jane, but she attacks Jane's veil, a symbol of marriage. Similarly, Mrs. Flint's hostile scrutiny of Jacobs provides Jacobs with some protection against the schemes of Dr. Flint. Jacobs describes Mrs. Flint as a cruel person who, "like many southern women, was totally deficient in energy. She had not strength to superintend her household affairs; but her nerves were so strong, that she could sit in her easy chair and see a woman whipped, till the blood trickled from every stroke of the lash" (12). At the same time, however, Jacobs repeatedly observes that "the power was still all in [Dr. Flint's] own hands. I pitied Mrs. Flint" (34). Brontë's and Jacobs's texts both suggest that despite the differences between the female slave and her mistress or the "mad" woman and the "sane," no woman is free in a patriarchal society.

THE ENEMY WITHIN

In patriarchal cultures such as nineteenth-century England and the United States, male-constructed legal and economic institutions attempt to deprive women of the power to effect social change, individually or collectively. In addition, every potential community of women is undermined from within, in a double sense. First, multiple antagonisms divide women from each other. Second, every woman is divided against herself, filled with conflict and contradictions; no woman is a unified subject. In poem #642 Emily Dickinson describes this self-division; the enemy within is the most difficult to conquer:

Me from Myself—to banish—
Had I Art—
Impregnable my Fortress
Unto All Heart—

But since Myself—assault Me—

How have I peace
Except by subjugating
Consciousness?

And since We're mutual Monarch
How this be
Except by Abdication—
Me—of Me?

In slave narratives and Gothic novels, we find protagonists who are simultaneously conformists and rebels, mediators of the patriarchal order and agents of social change. Mary Wollstonecraft wrote in *A Vindication of the Rights of Woman*, "I do not wish [women] to have power over men; but over themselves." To gain power over themselves, heroines must wage war against internal as well as external enemies.

Denied access to crucial social institutions and constricted by impossible and contradictory images of what women should be, the protagonists of female Gothic novels and slave narratives are trapped in tempests of conflicting emotions from which they cannot find release. Their external world appears to be a vast prison, and their internal world mirrors that reality. To maintain their sanity, to gain some control over their lives—in short, to survive—Gothic and slave heroines must understand multiple aspects of themselves in relation to other women.

In "A Narrative of the Life and Travels of Mrs. Nancy Prince" (1853), Prince movingly describes the inner torment of women who blame themselves for their own victimization. As children, Nancy and her sister Silvia are abused not only by whites but also by their stepfather. As "free" blacks in Massachusetts, the two girls must support themselves from a very young age. In 1816, when they are in their early teens, Silvia is "deluded" into a brothel in Boston. Nancy is "so distressed" when she learns of her sister's fate that she walks in the cold weather of early February from Salem to Boston to "rescue my lost sister" (13). Both sisters are morally repulsed by the "foul and unclean" life of "harlots"; when Silvia sees Nancy, she cries, "Nancy, O Nancy, I am ruined!" (14). Nancy, Silvia, and a male friend wielding a large cane fight their way out of the brothel, but Silvia is never able to escape from the inner torment produced by her "ruin." Years later when Prince is writing her narrative, she is still full of agony about the degradation of her sister. She pleads with the reader (and with herself) to understand that her sister's "soul is precious; she was very dear to me . . . and often protected me from the blows of an unkind step-father. She often said she was not fit to live, nor fit to die" (15). Silvia's tragic sense of worthlessness is a sign of the extent to which she internalized the dominant racist-sexist values of her society.

Like Silvia, Gothic heroines also are tormented by their internalization of patriarchal values. Female Gothic fiction is psychologically complex largely because it removes the boundaries between world and psyche that characterize "realism." Labyrinths, dungeons, and storms exist both in the material world and in the protagonist's mind. Wollstonecraft points to this blurring of inner and outer reality when her autobiographical heroine Mary asks herself: "Where am I wandering, God of Mercy! . . . she alluded to the wanderings of her mind. In what a labyrinth am I lost! . . . Wherefore am I made thus? Vain are my efforts—I cannot live without loving—and love leads to madness. . . . She looked for hope; but found none—all was troubled waters.—No where could she find rest" (62). For Mary, external troubles cannot match the internal strife she feels constantly. The narrator comments that when Mary contemplates a "tempestuous" storm out of doors, "the tempest in her soul rendered every other trifling—it was not the contending elements, but *herself* she feared!" (37).

In a famous letter discussing her views of Jane Austen, Charlotte Brontë reveals the primary aesthetic value of most female Gothic novelists: emotional intensity. She disliked reading Austen because Austen "ruffles her reader by nothing vehement, disturbs him [*sic*] by nothing profound: the Passions are perfectly unknown to her; she rejects even a speaking acquaintance with that stormy Sisterhood. . . . Jane Austen was a complete and most sensible lady, but a very incomplete, and rather insensible (not *senseless*) woman."[6] Unlike most female Gothic novelists, Austen diffuses emotional involvement in *Northanger Abbey* by her tone of detached irony. Typically, female Gothic novels not only depict emotional excess in their characters; they also evoke intense emotional responses in readers, even while the narrators are advocating the primacy of reason. Ann Radcliffe, Mary Wollstonecraft, Mary Shelley, and the Brontës all depict repression of emotion as evil, endorsing St. Aubert's advice to Emily in *The Mysteries of Udolpho*: "I would not annihilate your feelings, my child, l would only teach you to command them; for whatever may be the evils resulting from a too susceptible heart, nothing can be hoped from an insensible one; that . . . is all vice" (20). Gothic heroines pay for their emotional involvement in life by suffering from psychological paralysis, hypochondria, and madness. Indeed, because of the strictures patriarchal culture places on women, the strength of women's conflicting and inexpressible emotions often leads to an early death. Nonetheless, no female Gothic protagonist will accept a life devoid of emotional connectedness. Cold, calculating, "insensible" characters may gain a transitory form of power, but they are shown to be miserable and full of "vice," as St. Aubert predicts.

The central tension in female Gothic, as in much of women's literature, is the tension "between the opposed and moralized bastions of reason and feeling."[7] However, even the texts' warnings against passion are passionate. For example, Lady Laurentini of Udolpho is "a dreadful victim to unresisted passion" (659) who haunts Emily St. Aubert throughout Radcliffe's novel. After finally disclosing her identity and history, Laurentini passionately warns Emily to avoid passion: "Sister! beware of the first indulgence of the passions; beware of the first! Their course, if not checked then, is rapid—their force is uncontrollable—they lead us we know not whither—they lead us perhaps to the commission of crimes, for which whole years of prayer and penitence cannot atone!" (646). As Laurentini's manner of speaking suggests, passion may be dreaded, but it cannot be avoided.

In *Jane Eyre* and *Villette*, Charlotte Brontë created multiple female characters in order to assess various ways of dealing with the limitations patriarchal culture places on women. On the one hand are the Helen Burnses, too passive in the face of evil, too dedicated to solitary contemplation, to survive in this world. On the other hand are the Bertha Masons, driven mad by social penalties for assertive expressions of sexuality. Jane Eyre finds both models unacceptable, seeking desperately for a way to combine a meaningful intellectual life with a nondegrading expression of adult sexuality.

Although sexual passion may be the emotion most feared by Gothic heroines, other passions also appear dangerous. When Charlotte Brontë refers to "the stormy Sisterhood" of female passions, she includes a wide range of emotions: anger, joy, desire, pain, revenge. Erotic energy erupts throughout the texts: in descriptions of sublime landscapes, in characters' artistic endeavors (painting, music, writing, acting), and in characters' desires for conversational, communal, and sensual fulfillment. Anger at social injustice also seethes constantly under the textual surface, occasionally exploding and always threatening to disrupt the text, as in Brontë's "feminist manifesto" quoted above.

Another primary passion dramatized in both Gothic novels and slave narratives is passion for power. Although female authors of Gothic novels and slave narratives exposed the terrors of unchecked male power over women, they did not depict men and women, or blacks and whites, as essentially different in their desire for power. Gothic protagonists—Emily St. Aubert, Maria, Jemima, Frankenstein's creature, Catherine Earnshaw-Linton, Jane Eyre, Lucy Snowe—are all eager for the power to control their destinies, to speak, to voice desire. Similarly, the protagonists of female slave narratives are willing to fight the entire network of race, gender, and class oppressions to take some measure of control over their lives, to assert their humanity in the face of society's savagery. Furthermore, both genres forcefully dramatize the evils that result from human beings whose passion for power is focused not on power over self but on power over others.

In *The Mysteries of Udolpho*, all corrupt characters, whether male or female, are distinguished by their insatiable hunger for power over other people. Emily's first victimization comes at the hands of her aunt, Madame Cheron, to whose care she was entrusted by her father when he died. Madame Cheron's love of power is "her ruling passion, and she knew it would be highly gratified by taking into her house a young orphan, who had no appeal from her decisions, and on whom she could exercise without control the capricious humour of the moment" (112). Starved for power, Cheron exercises it greedily during the brief period she has it. She is petty, tyrannical, and antipathetic to the usual feminine virtues of silence and diffidence, virtues with which Emily is amply endowed. Contemptuous of her niece, Cheron informs Emily's lover, Valancourt: "I will take upon me to answer for her. . . . My will is hers" (138). Shocked by "the fearless manners" of her aunt, Emily reinforces her own submission to culturally sanctioned femininity, "shrink[ing] into the reserve, that would protect her from [her aunt's] absurdity" (118). To Emily at this point in the novel, "fearless manners" appear absurd in a woman.

Indeed, *The Mysteries of Udolpho* suggests that hunger for power *weakens* women because any woman who imagines she can maintain power in a society dominated by men is dangerously naive; she will be seen by men as a vain woman who needs to be forcibly put in her place. Cheron's obliviousness to the restrictions that patriarchal society places on aging women permits her to believe that men find her desirable when they say they do, even though she is middle-aged. Thus she accepts Montoni's marriage proposal without hesitation. After their marriage, she is quickly and mercilessly enlightened. Montoni exhibits no affection for his aging wife; in fact, he boldly brings his young mistress into their home. As a wife, the formerly loquacious Madame Cheron (now Madame Montoni) learns that her options as a married woman are quiet submission to her husband's will or death. She chooses death. Or, as the narrator states, "Madame Montoni was not of a nature to bear injuries with meekness, or to resent them with dignity"; therefore, she is imprisoned by her new husband in the east turret of his castle, where, he says, "you may understand the danger of offending a man, who has unlimited power over you" (190, 305). Burning with rage and resentment, Madame Montoni is consumed by a fever and dies in a few days. The narrator's last word on this power-hungry woman is that her brother, if he had lived, would have had much cause to regret having "committed his daughter to the care of a woman so weak as was Madame Montoni" (407). The major difference between Montoni and Madame Montoni is that he is socially empowered to enact his will, whereas she is rendered weak and, indeed, dead, by the attempt to enact hers.

Although Madame Montoni is represented as a dangerous model of womanhood in many respects, Emily eventually learns to emulate her firm resistance of Montoni. More thoroughly "fallen" than Madame Montoni, the Lady Laurentini of Udolpho is represented as a horrific example of a woman who fails to master her passions. As a young woman in love with the Marquis de Villeroi, Laurentini foolishly agrees to become his mistress before he fulfills his promise to make her his bride. After he breaks his promises and marries another woman, she considers killing herself or killing him but instead conspires with him to kill his wife, whose "gentle goodness and unimpassioned manners had ceased to please" him (658).

As usual, female characters are trapped in a hopeless situation. On the one hand, the Marquis poisons his wife because she is not sufficiently passionate to suit his taste. On the other hand, he originally chose not to marry Laurentini because she was too passionate, a quality enjoyable in a lover but unacceptable in a wife. Furthermore, after poisoning his wife, the Marquis again rejects Laurentini. He self-righteously chooses to see her only once, "and that was, to curse her as the instigator of his crime, and to say, that he spared her life only on condition, that she passed the rest of her days in prayer and penance" (659). The narrator assures us that the Marquis's conscience is tormented. However, he spends the rest of his life with his friends "amidst the tumult of war, or the dissipations" of various cities (659), a fate hardly comparable to that of Laurentini, who spends twenty years incarcerated in a convent as Sister Agnes, an insane nun, deprived of all friends and occupations, deprived even of her own name.

In Heathcliff and Catherine, Emily Brontë presents us with tormented characters who are neither villains nor heroes. Rather, they are victims of an unjust system who are socialized to undermine their own best selves. Although they rebel against and feel alienated by society, at crucial moments they become complicit in the conventions they despise. Through them, Brontë analyzes the catastrophic consequences of the intersection of gender and class oppression. Catherine fights against her father's tyranny, but she still longs for his love. She tries to save Heathcliff from degradation, but she cannot succeed. Both protagonists are disenfranchised—Catherine because of her gender and Heathcliff because of his lack of money and of family connections. Brontë also associates wealthy people's views of poverty with racism: Heathcliff is contemptuously labeled a "gipsy brat" and rejected for this racial otherness (77). Deprived of the emotional sustenance they provide for each other, Catherine and Heathcliff are rendered impotent against society, capable only of self-destruction.

An unusual and courageous aspect of Brontë's social analysis is that she does not gloss over the irremediable brutalization produced by a patriarchal, capitalistic society. Catherine and Heathcliff are heroic in that they are able to maintain at least a partial vision of life outside the strictures of their society. However, they cannot resist internalizing the values of the system they grew up in: Catherine learns to enjoy the fancy clothes, cleanliness, and social respect she gains at Thrushcross Grange, and Heathcliff learns to enjoy the power that comes from accumulating money and controlling other people.

Catherine and Heathcliff's susceptibility to destructive values is fostered in childhood, when they are poisoned by patriarchal pedagogy. In the Earnshaw household, the father makes decisions by which everyone must live. Even when his actions are charitable, as they appear to be when he adopts the homeless urchin Heathcliff, the father's tyranny undermines his benevolence. Unable to resist his power forthrightly, each member of the family bitterly resents his impositions, with dire consequences for all concerned. The wife "grumbles herself calm" and dies in less than two years (78, 79). The son, deterred from smoothly assuming his place in the patriarchal order, learns "to regard his father as an oppressor rather than a friend, and Heathcliff as a usurper of his father's affections and his privileges" (79). The daughter, unable to please her father, recognizes her kinship with Heathcliff, in whose usurpation of power she would like to participate. Like Jacobs's Dr. Flint, the patriarch of the Earnshaw household grows irritable and paranoid; "suspected slights of his authority nearly threw him into fits" (82). His rigid, repressive rule is self-defeating; he dies with his daughter literally laughing in his face.

Demanding expression of emotion yet aware of its dangers, Gothic heroines must carefully balance their steps over, as it were, a slippery mountain pass. Falling into the chasm on one side would mean a self-annihilating surrender to cold male power and logic, the fate of Jane Eyre had she married St. John Rivers. Falling into the chasm on the other side would mean a self-destructive surrender to uncontrollable passions, the fate of the madwoman in the attic, Bertha Mason, who smashes, burning, onto the pavement at Thornfield Hall. Like the narrator of Charlotte Perkins Gilman's Gothic short story "The Yellow Wallpaper," heroines in Gothic novels find everywhere the mangled remains of women who have tried to escape from the patriarchal order. "But nobody could climb through that pattern—it strangles so," observes Gilman's narrator (15).

Just as Emily Brontë shows in *Wuthering Heights* that the corruption of society ultimately will undermine the subversive potential of Catherine and Heathcliff's interclass, interethnic love, Harriet Wilson shows in *Our Nig* that racism and poverty can destroy the subversive potential of interracial marriage. Wilson's autobiographical novel opens with a description of her mother, Mag Smith, a young white woman with "a loving, trusting heart." Mag is "early deprived" of her parents and emerges "into womanhood, unprotected, uncherished, uncared for" (1). She becomes an easy victim to "the music of love" and is seduced, impregnated, and abandoned. The news of her "fall" follows her wherever she goes. Socially ostracized, she will accept any form of "drudgery" to support herself. Despite all her efforts, "every year her melancholy increased, her means diminished. At last no one seemed to notice her, save a kind-hearted African" named Jim. Jim befriends and eventually proposes marriage to Mag.

The marriage of an African man and a white woman was explosive material for Wilson to write about in 1859; certainly such a union held revolutionary potential. However, both Jim and Mag have internalized racism, just as Heathcliff and Catherine internalized the dominant values of their society. Jim proposes in an "abashed" manner: "Well,

Mag . . . you's down low enough. I do n't see but I've got to take care of ye.' Sposin' we marry! . . . I's black outside, I know, but I's got a white heart inside. Which you rather have, a black heart in a white skin, or a white heart in a black one?" (12). Jim is "proud of his treasure,—a white wife," and "love[s] Mag to the last," but she marries him only from dire necessity, feeling that she "has descended another step down the ladder of infamy" (13–15). She is "now expelled from companionship with white people; this last step—her union with a black— was the climax of repulsion" (15). Jim dies after a few years, and Mag becomes hardened by suffering. She eventually abandons her young children, whom she calls "black devils" (16). Thus although Wilson portrays interracial marriage sympathetically, she also represents it as contributing to a cycle of child abuse, abandonment, and economic exploitation.

Harriet Jacobs cites one example of an interracial relationship that is a significant act of insurrection. A daughter of a slaveholder rebels against her father by "selecting one of the meanest slaves on his plantation to be the father of his first grandchild. . . . Her father, half frantic with rage, sought to revenge himself on the offending black man; but his daughter, foreseeing the storm that would arise, had given him free papers, and sent him out of the state" (52). Jacobs states that she is citing this incident as an example of the corruption of slavery, which makes daughters desire to "exercise the same authority" as their fathers exercise over slaves. At the same time, Jacobs appears to enjoy the daughter's foresightedness and her heroic refusal to subordinate her sexuality to patriarchal control.

Enslaved women in the United States faced external threats more severe than those endured by Gothic heroines and southern white women. As William L. Andrews notes in *To Tell a Free Story*: "In the fictions of Ann Radcliffe, the Brontës, Charlotte Perkins Gilman, or the female Gothicists whom Ellen Moers has analyzed, there is no more stifling and oppressive 'imagery of entrapment,' 'enclosure,' and 'powerlessness' than that which appears in the middle chapters of Jacobs's autobiography" (258). The ultimate female Gothic event— one that conjures up women's worst fears of being buried alive— occurs in Jacobs's seven-year self-imprisonment in a tiny attic in her grandmother's house.[8] Despite this self-imprisonment, despite efforts unmatched by any Gothic heroine, Jacobs cannot escape sexual exploitation at the hands of one white man or another. With neither white skin nor middle-class respectability to protect her, an enslaved woman could not avoid sexual "falls" the way a Gothic heroine usually could. Less fanciful than Gilman's narrator, Jacobs truly sees everywhere the mangled remains of women who have been sexually exploited, tortured, and sold.

To add insult to injury, the fact that enslaved women were sexually victimized was often held up by white people as proof of black women's inherent moral inferiority. As Hazel Carby points out, when "measured against the sentimental heroines of domestic novels, the black women repeatedly failed the test of true womanhood because she survived her institutionalized rape, whereas the true heroine would rather die than be sexually abused" (34). Harriet Jacobs protested to her readers that "slave women ought not to be judged by the same standard as others" (56). Nonetheless, she faced a stern internal judge. Her narrative reveals pervasive anxiety about her liaison with Mr. Sands, the white lover she accepted in lieu of Dr. Flint.

Unlike most "fallen" Gothic female characters, Jacobs finds a place of redemption—in the arms of her daughter, Ellen. For many years, Jacobs writes, "my pent-up feelings had often longed to pour themselves out to some one I could trust" (189). Finally, although she feared losing Ellen's love, she "resolved to tell her something about her father" (188). To her surprise, her daughter "clasped me in her arms" and said, "I know all about it, mother. . . . I am nothing to my father, and he is nothing to me. All my love is for you" (188–89). Ellen's rejection of the dominant culture's racist-sexist valorization of "chastity" and "legitimacy" enables her to treat herself and her mother with respect and compassion. In this picture of a daughter's understanding and undiminished affection for her mother—in the embrace between two women—Jacobs offers hope that women will be able to liberate each other from the self-hatred that accompanies victimization.

DREAMS OF SOLIDARITY

The female Gothic and slave narrative genres diverge widely in the ways their authors represent visions of a better world. Gothic novelists could allow themselves hundreds of pages in which to dream about utopian possibilities, whereas slave narrators were expected to focus their brief narratives on exposing the horrors of slavery. Slave narratives were written with the immediate goal of improving the world by abolishing slavery—a goal towards which they contributed significantly. Gothic novels were not political in the same immediate sense. Furthermore, while slave narrators attempted primarily to envision a world of racial equality, female Gothic novelists attempted primarily to envision a world of sexual equality.

For slave narrators, solidarity or betrayal among women had immediate physical consequences: slaves were abused or protected, hidden or exposed, by other women on a daily basis. Many slaves risked their lives to protect and assist other slaves; the bonds of sisterhood and brotherhood were sometimes amazingly strong. When Frederick Douglass, "free" in the North, dreams of a home, he remembers "the society of my fellow-slaves. They were noble souls; they not only possessed loving hearts, but brave ones. We were linked and interlinked with each other. I loved them with a love stronger than any thing I have experienced since. . . . I believe we would have died for each other. We never undertook to do anything, of any importance, without a mutual consultation. We never moved separately. We were one" (*Narrative* 115). Similarly, Jacobs reveals at the end of her narrative that although life in the north has not fulfilled her dreams of human community, she consoles herself with memories of her "oppressed people," especially her "good old grandmother." These memories are "like light, fleecy clouds floating over a dark and troubled sea" (201).

In addition to dreaming of freedom for all slaves, many slave narrators long to be reunited with one particular loved one. Mary Prince expresses her longing for the husband from whom she has been forcibly separated, and Louisa Picquet tells her story in order to raise money to buy her mother out of slavery. Other slave narrators express little hope for human communities on earth; they dream instead of the Kingdom of God where peace and love will reign. In any case, the constraints of the antebellum slave narrative genre prevented writers from exploring in depth their dreams of a better world.

Nonetheless, in most cases the act of telling their tales was in itself an expression of the narrators' dreams of solidarity among white and black people. In particular, many black women who told their tales evoked the ideal of sisterhood between themselves, their enslaved sisters, and their white female audience. The black poet Sarah L. Forten emphasized the moral necessity of women's solidarity in 1871 when she addressed white women in the following manner:

We are thy sisters. God has truly said,
That of one blood the nations he has made.

> O, Christian woman! in a Christian land,
> Canst thou unblushing read this great command?
> Suffer the wrongs which wring our inmost heart,
> To draw one throb of pity on thy part!
> Our skins may differ, but from thee we claim
> A sister's privilege and a sister's name.[9]

Time and again Harriet Jacobs also appeals directly to the reader that she images as white and female. As Yellin observes, "*Incidents* was written and published to foster a community of women who would act to oppose slavery" (*Women and Sisters* 92).

Unlike slave narrators, the authors of Gothic novels were not intimately involved in racial warfare. However, they were, in different ways, fighting to survive in a white male-dominated world. Pained by the disempowerment of women in the patriarchal family yet still yearning for fulfillment within a human society, female writers of Gothic fiction recognized the importance of solidarity among women. In addition, they often were attracted to the utopian ideal of a separatist community of women. In the words of Julia Kristeva, a female countersociety is "constituted as a sort of alter ego of the official society, in which all real or fantasized possibilities for *jouissance* take refuge. Against the sociosymbolic contract, both sacrificial and frustrating, this countersociety is imagined as harmonious, without prohibitions, free and fulfilling" (27). Although many feminist critics like Kristeva associate this separatist ideal with modern radical feminism, in fact women's writing always—from ancient Greek poetry to contemporary science fiction—has explored the possibilities of a woman-centered social order. The first feminist essayist in England, Mary Astell (1666-1731), stressed the importance of friendships among women. Never marrying, she advocated establishing celibate female communities in which women and girls could live peacefully together, focusing their energies on education and good works.[10] Like Astell, female Gothic novelists repeatedly project fantasies of female communities. Ultimately, however, these communities are rejected as inviable and sometimes dangerous illusions.

The heroine of Mary Wollstonecraft's novel *Mary, A Fiction* (1788) initially longs for the type of female countersociety that Kristeva describes. Surrounded by masculine violence, the young Mary rejects men and forms primary emotional attachments to her mother and her friend Ann. She envisions a tantalizing world of female nurturance and companionship, but she quickly discovers that women are psychologically and materially trapped in the patriarchal order. As a consequence, they lack the resources to establish an alternative society. Her mother, who was educated to be "a mere machine" controlled by the will of first her father and later her husband, spoils her son, neglects her daughter, and dies quickly (1). Mary then looks to Ann for friendship, with feelings that "resembled a passion" (19). She often thinks about how "she loved Ann better than any one in the world— to snatch her from the very jaws of destruction—she would have encountered a lion. To have this friend constantly with her . . . would it not be superlative bliss?" (15). Ann, however, is desperately poor and too harassed by financial worries to have time to be the companion Mary needs. Ann's health is "undermined by care and grief," and she dies young (14).

While Ann is dying, Mary is grief stricken. Like many lovers in romantic fiction, she exclaims, "I cannot live without her!—I have no other friend." Her grief appears excessive and "strange" to the people around her; she is asked, "Have you not a husband?" (26). After Ann's death, social realities force Mary to abandon her dream of living among women. Her subsequent protests against social conventions make her an outcast from patriarchal society, but she cannot find a way to create an alternative order.

In 1827, Mary Shelley wrote to a friend that "the memory of my Mother has always been the pride and delight of my life; & the admiration of others for her, has been the cause of most of the happiness I have enjoyed" (*Letters* 2: 3–4), an astonishing statement considering that Wollstonecraft died shortly after giving birth to Mary and that her reputation was viciously attacked. Following in the footsteps of her mother, Mary Shelley was strongly attracted to the ideal of a harmonious community of women. In her comprehensive biography of Mary Shelley, Emily Sunstein traces the long history of Mary's intimate involvements with women and her desire for an enduring "community of outcast women" (268). This history has been ignored for the past 150 years largely because sexist and heterosexist literary critics have seen Mary as a satellite of her husband and have ignored the thirty years that Mary lived after Percy drowned. After his death, "Jane Williams gradually became Mary's second great love" (268). Mary wrote passionate letters to and about Jane, stating "She is in truth my all— my sole delight," describing her "Sweet loveliness" and her "perfections of grace and beauty" and praising the beauty of her "Notches" (female genitals) (qtd. in Sunstein 272). Mary was heartbroken when she discovered after several years that Jane was a duplicitous friend who spoke cruelly of Mary behind her back.

Despite her tremendous disappointment, Mary continued to attempt to build communities of women. For many years she "befriended a brilliant, bizarre social outcast, Mary Diana Dods," who was "a secret lesbian and sometimes transvestite" (Sunstein 273). Shelley and Dods concocted a "wild and wonderful" plan to rescue a secret unwed mother, Isabel Robinson. Dods posed as a man ("Mr. Sholto Douglass") and eloped with Robinson to Paris, where they spent two years together, after which "he" disappeared and "Mrs. Douglass" returned to England with her baby (280).

Although Mary Shelley had little money, she supported and sometimes lived with two sisters, Rosa and Julia Robinson. In the end, however, she found that her best efforts could not bring about the enduring intimate community she desired. Women's relationships were constantly undermined by the compulsory heterosexuality of Victorian England. In addition, Mary was trained from childhood to sacrifice herself for the happiness of others; as a consequence, she had difficulty establishing egalitarian relationships in which she could be nurtured as much as she nurtured her partner. In 1842 she concluded that "it is hazardous for a woman to marry a woman. . . . I struggled hard to retain personal independance [sic]" (Letters 3: 36).

Despite her courageous lifestyle, Mary Shelley was unwilling or unable to take the risks in writing that her mother had. She argued that "books do much—but the living intercourse is the vital heat. . . . If I have never written to vindicate the Rights of women I have ever befriended women when oppressed—at every risk I have defended and supported victims to the social system" (qtd. in Sunstein 342). Mary observed that her mother was severely punished for advocating women's rights and that her father and Percy purported to love all humanity but mistreated the human beings with whom they lived. After her radical "friend" Edward John Trelawny called her "a hurricane in petticoats," echoing Walpole's insult of Wollstonecraft as a "hyena in petticoats," it is not surprising that Mary said she did not have "a passion for reforming the world" and refused Trelawny's request to "write a pamphlet on women's rights for the Philosophical Radicals" (Sunstein 306, 341). Finally Mary chose to live her life according to the belief that no creed, theory, or political commitment is as important as how well one treats other people.

Alienated and hurt by the many social reformers with whom she was intimately connected, Mary Shelley learned at a young age to voice her rage, pain, and resentment only in imaginative forms. Most of her novels focus on relationships among male characters; she disguises herself as the monster, the absent mother, or the silent heroine. In *Mathilda*, her most shocking and personal novel, Mary exposed the abuse and violation to which she had been subjected by her father and Percy. However, she apparently did not want to admit to herself what she had done; she sent the manuscript to her father in 1820, "with a request that [he] would arrange for its publication" (Nitchie vii). Godwin, of course, found the story "disgusting and detestable" and refused to submit the manuscript for publication or to return it to Mary (Nitchie xi). It remained unpublished until 1959.

Unlike Mary Wollstonecraft and Mary Shelley, Ann Radcliffe appears to have spent her adult life in a fairly conventional marriage. We in fact know very little, however, about Radcliffe's private life, and her novels suggest that relationships with women were crucially important to her. In order to explore the potentialities of communities of women, Radcliffe set many sections of her novels in convents. In *The Italian*, she describes both the dreams and the nightmares that may result from a female countersociety. On the one hand, the Convent of Santa della Pieta is a beautiful haven of female love, companionship, and nurturance, governed justly by a benign matriarch. On the other hand, the Convent of San Stefano is a horrific mirror of the patriarchal order; in it, women are imprisoned and terrorized by power-hungry female agents of the patriarchy. In a world where women often have to choose the lesser of two evils, any institution governed by women can provide some refuge for female victims of masculine violence. Thus Ellena Rosalba's mother, Olivia, chooses incarceration in San Stefano, where nuns who displease the prioress may be starved to death, over life with her abusive husband (Fernando di Bruno, alias Father Schedoni). In turn, Ellena finds her lost mother within the walls of this convent, which compensates to some extent for the pain to which she is subjected during her imprisonment there.

During their moments of greatest desperation, Radcliffe's heroines see convents as refuges of relative peace and safety. Ultimately, however, Radcliffe presents these communities of women as almost as problematic as societies dominated by men; convents are, after all, part of the Catholic church and directly subject to the church's male hierarchy. When Radcliffe's heroines have the power to choose, they always choose the possibilities of life in the world at large over the conventual life. Convents, at their best and at their worst, are simply tightly restricted spaces from which men are physically but not ideologically absent. Radcliffe often represents the physical absence of men as highly desirable, but her texts also suggest that removing men from a small area does not fundamentally change the existing power system.

Near the end of Charlotte Brontë's *Villette*, Lucy Snowe states, "M. Emanuel [her lover] was away three years. Reader, they were the happiest three years of my life" (488). During these years, Lucy is financially secure and able to establish a school for girls. Just as Radcliffe contrasted the two convents in *The Italian*, Brontë contrasts Lucy's school with Madame Beck's school. Lucy is a more benign "directrice" than Madame Beck, but both schools are women-centered microcosms that provide some space in which women and girls can grow. This space is important, but it does not allow the freedom and fulfillment that Gothic heroines ultimately desire. Given extraordinarily good luck, Lucy is able to find satisfaction in her work, but sexual fulfillment remains beyond her reach, just as it remains beyond the reach of Madame Beck.

Female Gothic novels and slave narratives powerfully dramatize the need for solidarity among women. Both genres represent a "stormy Sisterhood" of passions between women and within each individual woman. Hoping for universal solidarity, readers find instead a complex web of intricate entanglements: desire, betrayal, love, anger, nurturance, and cruelty. The protagonists and authors of Gothic novels and slave narratives are often empowered to survive by the nurturance and support they receive from other women. Just as often, however, women's relationships are disrupted by, among other things, the social and psychological dynamics of racism, sexism, classism, and compulsory heterosexuality. When they are unable to depend on communities of women, female protagonists must explore multiple additional avenues of potential escape from their imprisonment and enslavement. The next chapter examines these avenues of escape.

4

MOMENTS
OF
ESCAPE

I never hear the word "escape"
Without a quicker blood
A sudden expectation,
A flying attitude!

I never hear of prisons broad
By soldiers battered down,
But I tug childish at my bars
Only to fail again!

Emily Dickinson

Tremble not before the free man, but before the slave who has chains to break.

Margaret Fuller

I N THE emotional climax of Alice Walker's *The Color Purple* (1982), Mr. —— (a nameless patriarch) laughs at Celie's first verbal act of self-determination, a curse of him. "Who you think you is? he say. You can't curse nobody. Look at you. You black, you pore, you ugly, you a woman. Goddam, he say, you nothing at all" (213). Claiming a power she does not understand, Celie again curses Mr. —— and declares "to everything listening: I'm pore, I'm black, I may be ugly and can't cook. . . . But I'm here" (214).

Like Shug, feminist critics may want to respond to Celie's act of self-assertion by saying "Amen. . . . Amen, amen" (214). But we also need to ask where Celie's ability to resist Mr. —— comes from. If, as most contemporary critical theorists argue, the self is socially constructed, how can marginalized people resist their marginalization? How can a woman like Celie (poor, black, and "ugly") claim mastery over language and curse the fathers if her self has been constructed within a racist, classist, misogynist culture? Indeed, how can *any* woman assert herself in opposition to the dominant ideological definitions of womanhood? These questions, which have troubled women writers since the eighteenth century, still constitute central issues for feminist theory.

Partial answers to these questions can be found by examining the contradictions and tensions within the dominant ideology. Although we are all to a large extent socially constructed, no ideological system is monolithic, impermeable, or static. Ideology is "both contested and always under construction"; it is "fissured by competing emphases and interests" and "always open to revision, dispute, and the emergence of oppositional formulations" (Poovey, *Uneven Developments* 3). Foucault has pointed to "the omnipresence of power: not because it has the privilege of consolidating everything under its invincible unity, but because it is produced from one moment to the next, at every point, or rather in every relation from one point to another. Power is everywhere; not because it embraces everything, but because it comes from everywhere" (93). Dominant ideologies or discourses may define a particular group as powerless, but that group will always resist the dominant definitions. As long as she or he is alive, every human being is a source of power, even though that power may be severely restricted.

The ideologies that have been built to justify the subjugation of women and enslaved men have depended on the notion that these human beings could be completely "made one" with their husbands and masters. In other words, dominant classes have defined women and slave men as intellectually inferior, subhuman creatures who exist as mere extensions of the patriarch's will. However, at the same time, masters have constantly stressed the need for women and enslaved men to obey, which implies that they have a will. The contradiction between viewing oppressed people as both naturally subordinate and perpetually disobedient is irresolvable in patriarchal ideology, and it has led to multiple problems and opportunities. For example, in the antebellum American South "the courts had to recognize the humanity—and therefore the free will—of the slave or be unable to hold him accountable for antisocial acts" (Genovese 29). History has shown continually that no amount of physical force or ideological mystification can permanently deprive a human being of his or her will. The power to choose—in fact, the inevitability of choice—is an inalienable part of being human. As Genovese argues, "The humanity of the slave implied his action, and his action implied his will. Hegel was therefore right in arguing that slavery constituted an outrage, for, in effect, it has always rested on the falsehood that one man could become an extension of another's will" (88).

The texts written by fugitive slaves between 1790 and 1865 reveal that the authors usually saw through the mystifications of southern paternalism. Indeed, the texts contain remarkably lucid accounts of how the system intertwined race, class, and gender oppressions. Ironically, the authors' clear comprehension of their social disempowerment often enables them to claim power—to declare war against slave owners and the system they represent. As Harriet Jacobs wrote, "I had not lived fourteen years in slavery for nothing. I had felt, seen, and heard enough, to read the characters, and question the motives, of those around me. The war of my life had begun; and though one of God's most powerless creatures, I resolved never to be conquered" (19). Jacobs is well aware that she is "one of God's most powerless creatures" within the system of patriarchal slavery, but she refuses to accept the "social death" designed for her. Although subjected constantly to her master's "stinging, scorching words; words that scathed ear and brain like fire," she refuses to allow her identity to be constructed within the confines of the dominant racial and sexual ideology. Instead, she declares that "when he told me that I was made for his use, made to obey his command in *every* thing; that I was nothing but a slave, whose will must and should surrender to his, never before had my puny arm felt half so strong" (18). By reading Flint's blatant assertion of power as a call to fight "the war of my life," Jacobs empowers herself.

Jacobs's narrative represents many heroic women, black and white, who fought their oppressors with physical strength, spiritual courage, linguistic dexterity, and astonishing creativity. Jacobs demonstrates a profound understanding of the multiple ways women are victimized. She shows, for example, that although black women were excluded from the definitions and rewards of "true (white) womanhood", they nonetheless were expected to be submissive, passive, and unquestioning. Slaveholders routinely beat, raped, and terrorized slave women in attempts to break their will. Yet, even in the face of these horrors, Jacobs suggests that it is self-defeating to see oneself as powerless and the oppressor as omnipotent; she insists that patriarchs' power is increased when women believe they cannot resist victimization.

Jacobs's insight, courage, and determination are succinctly expressed when she declares: "My master had power and law on his side; I had a determined will. There is might in each" (85). Before Yellin documented the events in Jacobs's narrative, generations of critics and historians believed that Jacobs's description of her war against her owner was too romantic and naive to be true. However, Jacobs's narrative, like most slave narratives, demonstrates that the human will is in fact a powerful force capable of resisting tremendous social pressure. The African Americans who wrote slave narratives did not acquire literacy merely to read "the signs of their enslavement. Through their labors of artistry, they attempted to transform" society (Blount 29). Their belief in their own power may have been "romantic," but it nonetheless enabled them to wage and to win many battles against the forces that oppressed them.

In order to resist the victimization that patriarchal ideology presents as inevitable for women, feminist writers have always worked both to understand how women are socially disempowered and to envision how women can take power. In other words, feminists must accurately measure the strength of the forces we are fighting against without giving way to paranoia and despair. Nineteenth-century antislavery feminists maintained a tension between critiquing their powerlessness and asserting their power by alternately "picturing themselves as chain-breaking liberators and as enchained slaves pleading for their own liberty" (Yellin, *Women and Sisters* 25). Similarly, Audre Lorde forcefully registers the simultaneous subjectivity and agency of women when she asserts that "within the war we are all waging with the forces of death, subtle and otherwise, conscious or not—I am not only a casualty, I am also a warrior" (41).

Oppressed people have always struggled against oppression; the long history of feminism is the history of women's resistance to subjugation. American slave women had to fight oppression on many fronts; therefore, "resistance was woven into the fabric of slave women's lives and identities" (Fox-Genovese 329). Resistance took many forms, as Fox-Genovese shows:

> The ubiquity of [slave women's] resistance ensured that its most common forms would be those that followed the patterns of everyday life: shirking, running off, "taking," sassing, defying. The extreme forms of resistance—murder, self-mutilation, infanticide, suicide—were rare. But no understanding of slave women's identities can afford to ignore them, for, if they were abnormal in their occurrence, they nonetheless embodied the core psychological dynamic of all resistance. The extreme forms captured the essence of self-definition: You cannot do that to me, whatever the price I must pay to prevent you.[1]

Like slave narratives, female Gothic novels also suggest that resistance can assume an almost infinite variety of forms; the meaning of any particular act depends on the context in which it is performed. Both genres affirm Foucault's assertion that "points of resistance are present everywhere in the power network. Hence there is no single locus of great Refusal, no soul of revolt, source of all rebellions, or pure law of the revolutionary. Instead there is a plurality of resistances, each of them a special case: resistances that are possible, necessary, improbable; others that are spontaneous, savage, solitary, concerted, rampant, or violent; still others that are quick to compromise, interested, or sacrificial" (96). The protagonists of slave narratives and Gothic novels often develop an acute sensitivity to multiple forms of resistance. They understand the potentially subversive meanings of apparently innocent and simple acts—a word, a gesture, or a tone of voice. Both genres affirm Fox-Genovese's point that acts of resistance are usually subtle, but both genres also represent heroines who, when pushed hard enough, will resort to extreme acts of violence.

Female Gothic novels and slave narratives evaluate various methods of resistance. First, they suggest that oppressed people must affirm themselves in opposition to the dominant ideology. Second, they explore how women can benefit from cross-dressing and "passing" (as male, white, and/or wealthy). Third, they suggest that women can sometimes exploit male competition for their own benefit. Fourth, they represent nature as potentially a force above and beyond white male-dominated social systems—a force women can turn to for refuge and strength. Finally, they attempt to "remember" a childhood self who was free from social constrictions and to reconstruct that self. This chapter explores these various ways of resisting.

THE PROBLEMATICS OF SELF-AFFIRMATION

In her recent novel, *Beloved*, Toni Morrison draws on and integrates the female Gothic and slave narrative traditions in order to explore the possibilities of women's resistance to the dominant order. Her story was inspired by a mid-nineteenth-century account of the actions of Margaret Garner, a slave who escaped from Kentucky with her children. When slave catchers found her and attempted to return her and her children to slavery, as they were empowered to do under the Fugitive Slave Act, Garner tried to kill her children rather than allow them to be enslaved again. She managed to kill one of them before she was stopped. As Morrison presents the story, the resistance of a woman like Garner (Sethe in the novel) begins when she allows herself to value other human beings (her children) and culminates when she is able to value herself. She needs to absorb Paul D's gentle message: "You your best thing, Sethe. You are" (273).

As a mother, Sethe refuses to accept the "natal alienation" and social death that the slaveholders' ideology assigned to slaves. However, the price of her resistance is high, perhaps too high. Ultimately, as Morrison said in an interview, the only person who could evaluate Sethe's method of resistance "would be the daughter she killed" (Darling 5). By introducing Sethe's dead daughter into the text, Morrison pulls together the representational power of the female Gothic and African American literary traditions.

For many fictional heroines between 1790 and 1865, as for Morrison's Sethe, the ultimate act of resistance against oppression is to choose death over powerlessness. Mary Shelley and Emily Brontë represent death as the only way that Frankenstein's creature, Catherine, and Heathcliff can escape from becoming agents as well as victims of patriarchal violence. Female Gothic novelists and slave narrators understood, however, that the deaths of subjugated peoples rarely change the power structure. In the eighteenth and nineteenth centuries, millions of Africans died fighting their captors or committing suicide, choosing physical death over social death. Millions more died without a choice in transit to the Americas.[2] White men were as little affected by these deaths as by the deaths of the Native Americans that they routinely slaughtered. Furthermore, female Gothic novels often reflect white women's anxiety and anger over the murders of thousands of people during the Inquisition and witch hunts in fifteenth-, sixteenth- and seventeenth-century Europe. It is no surprise, then, that many women writers advocated survival over suicide, suggesting that to choose life is a more powerful act of resistance than to choose death, when one has a choice. Although female Gothic novelists and slave narrators emphasize the horrifying aspects of women's lives, they courageously represent protagonists as capable of creating significant moments of escape from the strictures of patriarchal domination without resorting to suicide or murder. During these moments, protagonists often succeed in negotiating a life worth living, despite the costs of oppression.

By creating the matriarchal figure of Baby Suggs in *Beloved*, Morrison explores a form of resistance to oppression that is less absolute than infanticide or suicide. In a central passage, Baby Suggs preaches a sermon celebrating the power of oppressed human beings to affirm themselves in opposition to the dominant order. She exhorts black children, men, and women to laugh, to dance, and to cry. Then she tells them that "the only grace they could have was the grace they could imagine" (89).

> "Here," she said, "in this here place, we flesh; flesh that weeps, laughs; flesh that dances on bare feet in grass. Love it. Love it hard. Yonder they do not love your flesh. They despise it. They don't love your eyes; they'd just as soon pick em out. No more do they love the skin on your back. Yonder they flay it. And O my people they do not love your hands. Those they only use, tie, bind, chop off and leave empty. Love your hands! Love them. Raise them up and kiss them. Touch others with them, pat them together, stroke them on your face 'cause they don't love that either. *You* got to love it, *you*! An no, they ain't in love with your mouth. Yonder, out there, they will see it broken and break it again. What you say out of it they will not heed. What you scream from it they do not hear. What you put in it to nourish your body they will snatch away and give you leavins instead. No, they don't love your mouth. *You* got to love it. This is flesh I'm talking about here. Flesh that needs to be loved. Feet that need to rest and to dance; backs that need support; shoulders that need arms." (89)

In this passage Morrison emphasizes the interdependence of the material, the linguistic, and the psychological. Oppression is not merely a state of mind or a matter of discourse; human flesh—human existence—is at stake. Baby Suggs inspires her community to see that black people must cherish themselves in defiance of white definitions and violence.

Moments of escape like those Baby Suggs creates with her black community are necessary to survival. However, such moments are transitory. Baby Suggs is ultimately defeated by the cultural forces of racial hatred, violence, and sexual exploitation. She comes to believe that any vision of a world outside of white domination is an illusion and a lie; as a result of her disillusionment, "her faith, her love, her imagination and her great big old heart began to collapse" (89). Although tragic, Baby Suggs's final defeat does not eradicate the strength and joy her community drew from her moments of resistance.

Morrison never downplays the strength and hostility of the forces that threaten African Americans. Nonetheless, she insists that oppressed people need to affirm themselves, to love their bodies, to credit their needs—in short, to develop a value system that opposes the dominant ideology point by point, bone by bone. The dominant class may claim ownership of language and imagination, but the oppressed must not concede this claim. The only "grace" they will enjoy is the grace they are able to name, to claim for themselves.

The "Memoir of Old Elizabeth" (1863) dramatizes the difficulty of choosing life (or "claiming grace") when one is severed from one's human community. Elizabeth was born into slavery in Maryland in 1766. At the age of eleven, her master sent her to work on a farm several miles away from her family. As she describes it, "At last I grew so lonely and sad I thought I should die, if I did not see my mother" (Elizabeth 3). She runs away to visit her mother, but her mother is forced to return her to the new place. In the narrative recorded when she was ninety-seven years old, Elizabeth poignantly recalls that "at parting, my mother told me that I had 'nobody in the wide world to look to but God.' These words fell on my heart with pondrous weight, and seemed to add to my grief. I went back repeating as I went, 'none but God in the wide world'" (4). This experience of abandonment nearly kills her. For six months, she feels "as though my head were waters, and I could do nothing but weep. I lost my appetite" (4). Dying from sorrow, starvation, and overwork, the young Elizabeth finds grace in a religious experience that fills her "with sweetness and joy" and renews her desire to live (7).

By looking death in the face and finding within herself the power to survive without human help, Elizabeth buys a rare type of psychological freedom. She is liberated from social conventions because she claims access to an authority higher than white men. At the age of thirty she is freed by a master who "did not think it right to hold slaves for life" (8). Soon thereafter, she opens a Bible and reads, "Gird up thy loins now like a man, and answer thou me. Obey God rather than man" (9). She decides that she has been called to preach, and she defies restrictions of race, gender, education, and age to do so. From the age of forty-two to eighty-seven, she preaches throughout the northern states and Canada, resisting church officials, policemen, and public opinion. As she says, "The people there would not believe that a coloured woman could preach. And moreover, as she had no learning, they strove to imprison me because I spoke against slavery: and being brought up, they asked by what authority I spake? and if I had been ordained? I answered, not by the commission of men's hands: if the Lord had ordained me, I needed nothing better" (17). Religion is a powerful weapon for Elizabeth in her fight to claim a place in the world. Patriarchs may be mighty but God is omnipotent, and she claims direct access to Him. She gains a considerable following among poor black "sisters" who understand and are inspired by her route to power. White folk and elders of the church are indignant that a black woman would take it upon herself to speak; they repeatedly declare that her "meetings must be stopped, and that woman quieted" (12). But Elizabeth "was not afraid of any of them," and she continues to preach for forty-five years. Her mastery of the spoken word is so powerful that she confounds all her enemies.[3]

Ann Radcliffe was born in 1764, two years before "Old Elizabeth." Because Radcliffe was white, comfortably middle-class, and nominally free, she had access to institutions of education and publishing that were closed to Elizabeth. Radcliffe was able to develop her social analyses in long novels that were published in the 1790s, whereas Elizabeth had to summarize ninety-seven years of life in only nineteen short pages dictated to an amanuensis and published in 1863. While Radcliffe revealed little to the world about her personal life, Elizabeth did not even claim a last name—a complex gesture that simultaneously signals a violent severance from family connections, a bold refusal to be identified by a father or a master, and an ironic connection to royal naming (the other Elizabeths who need no family name). The linguistic traditions that Elizabeth and Radcliffe worked within developed partly in response to the different levels of access that British women and African American people had to institutions of power. Elizabeth became an eloquent foremother in the African American tradition of oratory that Toni Morrison honors in creating the character of Baby Suggs, whereas Radcliffe became a groundbreaking novelist in the tradition of British women's literature. Despite the differences in their modes of storytelling, both women's stories plot the ways women can survive in a male-dominated world.

Radcliffe knew that suffering was unavoidable for women, regardless of class or temperament, and she seriously evaluated various strategies of resistance. She suggested that a heroine should be "determined, since she must suffer, to suffer, if possible, with firmness and dignity" (*Italian* 68). In a famous encounter in *The Mysteries of Udolpho*, Emily says to Montoni:

> "You may find, perhaps, Signor . . . that the strength of my mind is equal to the justice of my cause; and that I can endure with fortitude, when it is in resistance of oppression."

> "You speak like a heroine," said Montoni, contemptuously, "we shall
> see whether you can suffer like one." (381)

Although this passage may be read as meta-melodrama, highlighting
the predictability of artistic conventions, it also expresses a central insight of female Gothic: a man's melodrama will become a woman's
reality.

In a similarly melodramatic but insightful passage in the first chapter of *Jane Eyre*, Jane begins her critique of male domination. Verbally
and physically abused by her cousin John, the child Jane exclaims,
"Wicked and cruel boy! . . . You are like a murderer—you are like
a slave-driver—you are like the Roman emperors!" (43). She is punished for this speech by being beaten by John and thrown into the red
room by Mrs. Reed, but nonetheless Brontë affirms Jane's naming of
oppression as essential to her personal growth. Because Jane is poor
and female, she must resist the dominant class and gender ideologies
in order to maintain the self-respect necessary for survival.

Often, like Frankenstein's creature and "Old Elizabeth," the protagonists of Gothic novels and slave narratives are alone in the world,
deprived of emotional sustenance and denied their own reason. Emily
Brontë suggests in her poem "To Imagination" that this social alienation forces women to envision an alternative interior world: "So hopeless is the world without, / The world within I doubly prize." After
recognizing the horror that exists in the social world, heroines must
learn to affirm themselves as human beings with valid desires and to
explore within themselves the inner space that Dickinson called the
"Undiscovered Continent." In other words, because patriarchal society
does not nurture women, we must emotionally reconstitute ourselves.
In the central emotional crisis in *Jane Eyre* (Jane's decision to leave
Rochester), Jane answers her question, "Who in the world cares for
you?" with the affirmation, "*I* care for myself. The more solitary, the
more friendless, the more unsustained I am, the more I will respect
myself" (344). Because she values herself, she finds the strength to
resist subjugation to Rochester.

Jane's self-affirmation is a crucial element of her agency; she autho-
rizes herself to act. Her self-affirmation does not, however, come from
a complete emotional void; earlier in the novel she received important,
although transient, moments of affirmation from other characters,
notably Helen Burns, Miss Temple, and even Rochester himself. One
cannot affirm oneself effectively if one has been deprived of every form

of external affirmation; one cannot emotionally reconstitute oneself in utter isolation, deprived of all tools and materials. Frankenstein's creature experienced abandonment from the moment of his awakening, and Shelley's novel eloquently expresses the devastating effects of his unmitigated emotional deprivation. The creature must force Frankenstein to connect with him, because even Frankenstein's abuse is more useful to the creature than his neglect. Mary Shelley once wrote that "however perilous the journey from slavery to liberty, it must be attempted and persevered in" (qtd. in Sunstein 323). In myriad ways, literary and personal, Shelley rebelled throughout her life against the ideology that imprisoned nineteenth-century women. However, her writings, particularly *Frankenstein*, reveal her to be fully aware of how costly "the journey from slavery to liberty" could be.

Often in their struggle for survival female Gothic heroines and slave narrators must not only learn to recognize evil and to affirm themselves, but they must also acquire some of the traits that patriarchal ideology represents as "natural" for women. Those characters who, like Catherine in *Wuthering Heights* or Madame Montoni in *Udolpho*, are unwilling or unable to conform do not survive. Those heroines who do survive must learn the ancient stoic (or the seventeenth-century Puritan) lesson of "how much more valuable is the strength of fortitude than the grace of sensibility" (*Udolpho* 214). Emily St. Aubert, for example, learns the value of silent, disguised resistance, determining to herself that "I will not indulge in unavailing lamentation, but will try to endure, with firmness, the oppression I cannot elude" (214).

In *The Mysteries of Udolpho* a debate between Madame Montoni and Emily about the best way to deal with an abusive husband dramatically illustrates a conflict between active and passive modes of resistance. In this discussion, which occurs after violent attempts by Montoni to take over his wife's property, Madame Montoni declares, "I am determined no power on earth shall make me [sign away my property]. Neither will I bear all this tamely. He shall hear his true character from me; I will tell him all he deserves, in spite of his threats and cruel treatment" (281). Madame Montoni's vehement refusal to submit to her husband's evil designs against her person and her property may appear noble to the reader, but it dismays Emily, who has been well trained by her father in the passive feminine virtues of prudence, patience, and endurance, qualities which conform to the traditional ethic of Christian martyrdom. Culturally conditioned to be "modest" (timid), Emily focuses on the very real dangers of self-assertion. She advises her aunt to be prudent and conciliatory because "your reproaches, however just, cannot punish him, but they may provoke him to further violence against you" (282). Madame Montoni contemptuously replies, "Conciliate indeed! I tell you, niece, it is utterly impossible; I disdain to attempt it" (282).

During this conversation Emily is "shocked to observe the perverted understanding and obstinate temper of Madame Montoni" (282). Nonetheless, after Madame Montoni's death Emily grows to appreciate the nobility of her aunt's active mode of resistance. Madame Montoni's privileged position as a financially independent member of the upper class enabled her to scorn the middle-class ideal of feminine meekness, but it did not enable her to evade the social consequences of resisting her husband's will. Emily's resistance to Montoni becomes as active and as wholehearted as her aunt's; however, in order to survive, Emily learns to mask her inner rebellion with an outward appearance that conforms as much as possible to patriarchal ideals of feminine quietness and passivity. In this manner Radcliffe enables Emily not only to thwart Montoni's plans but also to outlive him, whereas Madame Montoni pays with her life for her rebellion against Montoni.

In *The Italian*, written three years after *The Mysteries of Udolpho*, Radcliffe created a heroine bolder than Emily, one who protests actively against oppression as soon as she encounters it. Like Jane Eyre, Ellena Rosalba uses her inner resources to fight against apparently hopeless circumstances. She repeatedly finds that "the pride of conscious worth revived her courage and fortified her patience" (68).[4] While Emily fights for control of her body and her property largely for Valancourt's sake, Ellena judges and fights for herself. "'It is I only, who am injured,' said she to herself, 'and shall the guilty oppressor triumph, and the innocent sufferer sink under the shame that belongs only to guilt! Never will I yield to a weakness so contemptible. The consciousness of deserving well will recall my presence of mind, which, permitting me to estimate the characters of my oppressors by their actions, will enable me also to despise their power'" (68). Ellena's mother and aunt suffered greatly at the hands of men; therefore, they taught Ellena to recognize evil when she sees it. Although understanding evil does not free Ellena from external injustice, it does liberate her from the self-doubt and low self-esteem that often paralyze oppressed people. Like many heroines in Gothic novels and slave narratives, Ellena learns to affirm her "consciousness of deserving well," and this self-affirmation empowers her to resist her oppressors.

CROSS-DRESSING AND PASSING

White women and enslaved African Americans could not avoid occasionally reflecting on how much easier their lives would have been if they had been born male, white, or both. Mary Wollstonecraft's heroine in *The Wrongs of Woman* wonders explicitly: "Why was I not born a man, or why was I born at all?" (139). Reflections like this sometimes lead oppressed people to stifle their own personalities and to live vicariously through their fathers, brothers, sons, or masters. White middle-class women often attempted to gain or maintain a materially comfortable life by identifying with the interests of financially secure fathers or husbands. Similarly, slaves often took pride in being identified with a wealthy and powerful master (Douglass, *Narrative* 44; Genovese 113–58). However, Gothic novels and slave narratives show that some protagonists subverted the system by taking identification to its logical extreme: women presented themselves to the world as men and blacks assumed the appearance of whites. These disguises were psychologically hazardous, but sometimes they were effective stratagems in the fight against oppression. Their success highlights the inherent artificiality of gender and racial constructs.

Escaping from oppression usually requires protagonists to assume multiple disguises; Harriet Jacobs is representative in that she, on various occasions, adopts a pseudonym, dresses as a sailor (111–12), sends her enemy false information about her whereabouts, and pretends to be a wife traveling to meet her husband (157). The most dramatic instance of cross-dressing and passing, however, is portrayed in the narrative written by Ellen and William Craft, *Running a Thousand Miles for Freedom; or, The Escape of William and Ellen Craft from Slavery* (1860). As slaves in antebellum Georgia, William and Ellen Craft were "haunted for years" by "the mere idea that we were held as chattels, and deprived of all legal rights—the thought that we had to give up our hard earnings to a tyrant, to enable him to live in idleness and luxury— the thought that we could not call the bones and sinews that God gave us our own: but above all, the fact that another man had the power to tear from our cradle the new-born babe and sell it in the shambles like a brute" (271). In 1848 they devised a plan of escape that involved overcoming three major obstacles: race, gender, and illiteracy.[5] Ellen Craft, a fair-skinned "black" woman, disguises herself as a white male slaveholder. To hide the fact that she cannot write, she pretends to have a broken arm that has to be held in a cast. By claiming whiteness, maleness, and literacy, Ellen gains access to the central bastions of social power. William accompanies Ellen as "his" slave, and in eight days they successfully pull off the ruse and escape to "freedom" in the North.

The narrator of the story is William Craft. Throughout his exciting, witty description of the escape, he uses masculine pronouns to refer to his wife, whom he calls "my master." He delights in social satire; for example, he ridicules the convention of love at first sight when some young ladies fancy themselves in love with "my master." The ladies busy themselves attempting to make the supposedly invalid young gentleman comfortable. After they think "he" has fallen asleep, "one of them gave a long sigh, and said, in a quiet fascinating tone, 'Papa, he seems to be a very nice young gentleman.' But before papa could speak, the other lady quickly said, 'Oh! dear me, I never felt half so much for a gentleman in my life!' To use an American expression, 'they fell in love with the wrong chap'" (303).

Through their use of irony and satire, the Crafts demystify the dominant ideology. One of their main points is that "he who has the power, and is inhuman enough to trample upon the sacred rights of the weak, cares nothing for race or color" (272). They repeatedly emphasize that although people who oppress other people develop ideological systems such as racism to mystify the relation of domination, their desire for power cannot be contained within the boundaries they construct. The antebellum American South provided ample evidence that the slaveholders' desire for power could not be contained within the construct of race. Throughout their narrative, the Crafts emphasize the instability of racial slavery, warning white readers that if, like many slaves, Ellen Craft could pass as "white," the converse is also possible: "white" people without a trace of African blood in their veins could be enslaved. Indeed, they cite several examples of cases where southerners enslaved white Europeans. It was routine, of course, for white men to enslave their own "black" children, but some "worthless white people" also sold "their own free children into slavery" (274).

Many slave narratives echo the Crafts' warning about the instability of racial boundaries. William Wells Brown describes seeing a young woman who was "perfectly white, with straight light hair and blue eyes," on her way to be sold at the New Orleans market (188). Everyone stares at her—not because she is white and enslaved, but because of "her almost unparalleled beauty" (189). He also describes a white boy named Burrill who worked to help his impoverished mother support the family. His employer took him on a trip from Saint Louis to New Orleans and sold him into slavery, then told the mother that the boy had died of yellow fever (202).

Although more tentative in their insights than the authors of slave narratives, Gothic novelists also represent gender, class, and race boundaries as artificial and volatile. Charlotte Brontë's novels persistently explore the benefits and dangers of cross-dressing; Shirley Keeldar often dresses like a man, Rochester disguises himself as a female gypsy, and so on. Cross-dressing is particularly prevalent in *Villette*, Brontë's masterful exposition of the instability of perceived reality. When Lucy Snowe is asked to play "a man's part" in a theater production, she begrudgingly accepts, on the condition that she will retain "her woman's garb" underneath the male costume. For Lucy, the role is "somehow suggestive"—she suddenly feels "resolute to win and conquer" (136). Instead of pitying a rejected male lover, she "hardened [her] heart, rivalled and outrivalled him" (136). She relishes the role for one night; playing a man enables her to discover delightful sources of courage, strength, and desire within herself. The next day, however, she reflects on her position as a poor woman in a classist patriarchal society. She believes she can be nothing more than "a mere looker-on at life: the strength and longing must be put by" (137); therefore, she resolves never again to play a man's part. But despite her apparent (and deceptive) resignation at the end of this passage, dressing as a man enables her to escape for a few hours from the constrictions that society places on women.

In *A Room of One's Own*, Virginia Woolf describes her anger at being denied access to the library at "Oxbridge" because she is a woman. She reads "the shut doors of the library" as a sign of women's general exclusion from the dominant culture, and she thinks about "how unpleasant it is to be locked out" (24). On second thought, Woolf concludes that "it is worse to be locked in" (24). A similar insight is expressed by Louisa Picquet when she tells the story of her first love, a man who escapes from slavery only to become trapped in secrecy and lies by marrying a white woman in New York. When Picquet discovers him twenty years later, he says that he and his wife have four children, and that no one suspects that he is "of African descent" (41). Nonetheless, he constantly lives with the knowledge that if his secret gets out, "it might break up a family, or one of our white citizens in New York might be remanded back to slavery" (41). In the meantime, he is severed from the black community and surrounded by the

racism of whites. Picquet does not comment on this man's decision
to pass, but early twentieth-century African American novelists like
James Weldon Johnson (*The Autobiography of an Ex-Colored Man*, 1912),
Jessie Fauset (*Plum Bun*, 1928) and Nella Larsen (*Passing*, 1929) suggested that cross-dressing and passing could be soul-destroying acts
when one attempted to escape oppression by remaining permanently
in the enemy's camp.

The narrative of Ellen and William Craft represents passing as a
dangerous and exhausting game. Ellen plays the part of a white gentleman with astonishing grace, but William states that once they reached
freedom, Ellen "burst into tears, leant upon me, and wept like a child.
The reaction was fearful. . . . she was in reality so weak and faint
she could scarcely stand alone. . . . After my wife had a little recov-
ered herself, she threw off the disguise and assumed her own apparel"
(314–15). In general, female Gothic novelists and slave narrators do
not advocate permanently joining the ranks of the oppressors. Nonetheless, cross-dressing and passing are represented as effective tools of
resistance when adopted for a short period of time. Ellen and William
Craft's courage to transgress race, gender, and class lines enables them
to escape physically from southern slavery and to begin the process of
intellectual liberation (their first priority after they reach the North
is to learn to read and write). Lucy Snowe has less at stake than the
Crafts, but her hours of acting a man's role are represented as crucial
to her psychological growth.

EXPLOITING MALE COMPETITION

Another strategy that protagonists employ in women's slave narratives
and Gothic novels to gain some control over their lives is exploiting the
competitiveness and jealousy that patriarchal culture fosters among
men. In other words, the texts suggest that women can improve their
chances of survival by recognizing how the social order works and,
whenever possible, using it against itself.

In *Incidents in the Life of a Slave Girl*, Harriet Jacobs describes her
struggle against Dr. Flint as "the war of my life" (19). In this war,
she will use any weapon she can find. She recognizes that she is "one
of God's most powerless creatures," but she courageously "resolve[s]
never to be conquered" (19). She will endure almost any physical and
psychological suffering rather than concede defeat. One of her bold-

est strategies is to exploit Flint's jealousy of other men. This strategy produces a great deal of anxiety in Jacobs; its psychological toll is such that years later, when she is nominally free and safe in the North, her writing manifests substantial uneasiness about it.

Jacobs delineates what is at stake in her war against Flint with remarkable insight and clarity. The problem she faces is precisely the problem discussed at the beginning of this chapter: how can a woman who is socially constructed as powerless claim power? Flint has "law and power" on his side when he tells Jacobs that she was "his property; that [she] must be subject to his will in all things." Jacobs is stymied: "My soul revolted against the mean tyranny. But where could I turn for protection?" (27). Over and over again, Jacobs asks herself and the reader where she can find the power to resist Flint. Her "mistress, who ought to protect the helpless victim, ha[d] no other feelings towards her but those of jealousy and rage" (27–28). Jacobs could not discuss the sexual nature of Flint's advances with her grandmother, because the grandmother was frighteningly stern about sexual matters. Furthermore, "Dr. Flint swore he would kill me, if I was not as silent as the grave" (28). Jacobs finally realizes that Flint's power is limited by his jealousy of other men. He will not send her to his plantation because "his son was there. He was jealous of his son; and jealousy of the overseer had kept him from punishing me by sending me into the fields to work" (41).

Despite the jealousies that constrain him, Flint's persecutions are unremitting. When he begins to build a small house four miles outside town to seclude Jacobs in, she becomes desperate. She says, "I would do any thing, every thing, for the sake of defeating him. What *could* I do? I thought and thought, till I became desperate, and made a plunge into the abyss" (53). The "abyss" Jacobs plunges into is a sexual liaison. To gain protection and to revenge herself against Flint, she accepts as a lover a white man named Mr. Sands. Sands is an influential, wealthy citizen in town who provides Jacobs with some protection from Flint's attentions. She has two children with him, and she has the pleasure of seeing Flint enraged by his own impotence.

Jacobs's courage in recounting this story to a white Victorian audience is as remarkable as her courage in living it. She states, "I knew what I did, and I did it with deliberate calculation" (54). She also says that people who "are free to choose" should not judge those whose options are severely restricted. She accepted Sands because "it seems less degrading to give one's self, than to submit to compulsion. There is something akin to freedom in having a lover who has no control over you, except that which he gains by kindness and attachment" (55). Jacobs expresses discomfort with her actions; her "self-respect" has been jeopardized (54). Despite the psychological costs, however, the strategy of playing men against each other achieves important results for Jacobs. Flint is frustrated, and, although Sands reneges on promise after promise, Jacobs gains some protection for herself and her children for several years.

Like Jacobs, female Gothic novelists represent women's exploitation of men's competition and jealousy as a dangerous but often effective strategy in the war against oppression. Ann Radcliffe suggests that because patriarchal law is committed to protecting the rights of more than one man, women can occasionally protect themselves by asserting the priority of one man's claims over the claims of another man. Like most female Gothic novelists, Radcliffe suggests that when a heroine cannot avoid being used as an object of exchange between men, she should attempt to align herself with the most humane man available.

In *Udolpho*, when Emily St. Aubert is besieged by the demands of Montoni, she strengthens her will to resist him by reminding herself that Valancourt's claims are more legitimate. When Montoni and his allies attempt to appropriate her language, her person, and her property she struggles to preserve herself for Valancourt. This effort is valorized by patriarchal ideology, which is committed to preserving the value of women as objects of exchange between men. Within the patriarchal system, Emily has been legitimately exchanged between her father (St. Aubert) and Valancourt. Radcliffe makes the nature of this exchange very explicit: the ill, aging St. Aubert is rescued from several dangerous situations by the young, handsome Valancourt; in return, St. Aubert smiles upon Valancourt's courtship of Emily.[6]

Because Emily has already been exchanged between men, Montoni's designs upon her constitute an illegitimate usurpation of other men's rights. Montoni's habit of overstepping the legal limitations of his power ultimately threatens the social order that empowered him in the first place. As Radcliffe presents it, however, Montoni's power is inherently illegitimate because it is founded on his appropriation of a female cousin's estates. If this cousin (Laurentini) were to appear, he would lose all claim to Udolpho. He is safe only because she is buried alive in a convent. In other words, the power operating in the castle of Udolpho derives from repressing a woman's rights, and the resurrection of this woman could lead to the collapse of the entire estate, as

Poe's house of Usher collapses when Madeline escapes from her tomb. Significantly, Radcliffe does not let Laurentini arise to claim her rights. More realistic than Poe, Radcliffe depicts women as unable to punish the men who violate them. Montoni can only be punished by *men* for his violations of *their* rights. (When Montoni threatens the security of the Italian Senate, the senators protect themselves by executing him.)

Searching for avenues of escape from the patriarchal order, then, Ann Radcliffe showed how women could benefit at times from men's preoccupation with competition. However, unlike Harriet Jacobs, Radcliffe never represents her heroines as consciously manipulative. They can maintain a rather pristine purity because they have a benevolent author-god who is determined to protect their virtue. Jacobs has no such resource; her analysis of her options is grounded in historical experience. When she cunningly outwits Flint, she wonders, "Who can blame slaves for being cunning? They are constantly compelled to resort to it. It is the only weapon of the weak and oppressed against the strength of their tyrants" (100–101).

In contrast to both Jacobs and Radcliffe, Emily Brontë depicts competition between men as destructive for both men and women. The fight of father against sons and sons against each other divides Heathcliff from Catherine, and Catherine's attempts to negotiate the competing demands of Edgar and Heathcliff result in disaster. Heathcliff's participation in the male competition for domination degrades and brutalizes him. His initial rebellion with Catherine against patriarchy is transformed into "competition for control of the patriarchy" (Restuccia 264). Heathcliff allows his desire for revenge against the classist, patriarchal system to take precedence over his alliance with Catherine. According to Gilbert and Gubar, Heathcliff "realizes that in order to subvert legitimacy he must first impersonate it; that is, to kill patriarchy, he must first pretend to be a patriarch" (297). But more than pretence is involved; Heathcliff *is* a patriarch in the second half of the novel, and this typical Oedipal transformation by which the rebellious son becomes the tyrannical father is as self-defeating as Catherine's decision to marry Edgar.

Catherine is sufficiently insightful early in the novel to recognize that since Heathcliff has been degraded by the system, it "would degrade [her] to marry Heathcliff, now" (121). She does not see that marrying Edgar Linton is also degrading; her shortsightedness in this respect shows that she is already complicit with and diminished by patriarchal values. Catherine and Heathcliff are both rebels against the dominant English gender and class ideologies, yet they have internalized and become complicit in the systems that degrade them. Their only hope of escape lies in recognizing their shared disenfranchisement and fighting together. Through most of the novel, their internalization of patriarchal values divides them along lines of gender and class and undermines their resistance.

Before her death, Catherine realizes that she has assumed a false and self-alienating role in society but, as she says, "If I've done wrong, I'm dying for it. It is enough!" (198). Torn between the conflicting needs and desires of various men, she, unlike Radcliffe's heroines, cannot simply choose the "right" one and live happily ever after. Brontë cannot envision any route for her heroine's physical survival. Catherine's choice to commit suicide is a final attempt to assert control over her life. She determines to escape from the "shattered prison" of her body "into that glorious world, and to be always there" (196).

Dying, Catherine is able to forgive herself and Heathcliff for their failure to sustain a united struggle against the conventional world, but Heathcliff protests: "I forgive what you have done to me. I love *my* murderer—but *yours*! How can I?" (198). For eighteen years, he attempts to master the system that killed Catherine. Finally, he attains Catherine's transcendental vision and comes to believe that "Catherine was there: not under me, but on the earth. A sudden sense of relief flowed, from my heart, through every limb. I relinquished my labour of agony, and turned consoled at once, unspeakably consoled. Her presence was with me" (321). With this vision, his antipathy to patriarchal, capitalistic values reemerges. He sees the futility of competing for control of a system that he despises; he relinquishes his patriarchal role and reasserts his rebellious spiritual energy. Like Catherine, Heathcliff discovers that his existence is incompatible with nineteenth-century English culture. His only hope for psychic survival is to leave the material world and to join Catherine in a transcendental sphere, "that glorious world."

SEEKING REFUGE IN NATURE

When the protagonists of female Gothic novels and slave narratives are exhausted by their fight against oppression, they look to a higher power for respite. Sometimes the texts label that higher power "God," as in the case of "Old Elizabeth." More often, they name it "nature."

Catherine and Heathcliff must die in order to join Emily Brontë's concept of a transcendental nature, but most Gothic novels and slave narratives represent nature as a life force that can enable human beings
to survive in *this* world.

Nature is typically represented in patriarchal ideology as a tempera-
mental woman who needs to be penetrated and tamed. During the
past 150 years, when life on earth has become threatened by human
pollution and technology, Mary Shelley's dramatization of the power-
hungry, life-hating scientist who rids his world of women and violates
nature has become a resonant cultural symbol. Female Gothic novelists and slave narrators typically represent nature not as a dumb object
to be conquered but as a transcendental force above and beyond the
might of men. Humanity is represented as merely one small part of
nature; the authors emphasize that nature is much larger and more
enduring than human constructs. Time and again the protagonists of
Gothic novels and slave narratives seek refuge in the parts of nature
that are not controlled by men, such as forests and swamps.

In keeping with the spirit of Romanticism, Gothic heroines sometimes regenerate themselves emotionally by contemplating sublime
landscapes—rugged mountains, tumultuous seas, brilliant sunsets.
Years before Wordsworth, Ann Radcliffe celebrated the liberating
power of sublime nature in evocative poetic language. Mary Poovey
observes that "in her romances Radcliffe investigates specifically the
paradoxical role sensibility plays in simultaneously restricting women
and providing them power and an arena for action" ("Ideology" 311).
Although overdeveloped sensibility sometimes leads protagonists to
paralyzing emotional excesses, Radcliffe's heroines all possess "the
grace of sensibility" that enables them to appreciate the wonders and
the power of nature. Overall Radcliffe suggests that sensitivity to
nature is essential for human beings' moral survival.

In her representations of nature, Radcliffe uses the aesthetic of the
sublime that Edmund Burke articulates in *A Philosophical Enquiry into
the Origin of Our Ideas of the Sublime and Beautiful* (1759), but she revises
his aesthetic in one important way. Burke describes the sublime as a
masculine force with foundations in "whatever is qualified to cause
terror," as opposed to the beautiful, which is a feminine phenomenon
derived from pleasure (131). Beauty induces affection, tenderness, and
love, "but love approaches much nearer to contempt than is commonly
imagined" (51, 67). In contrast to Burke, Radcliffe represents the sublime "as a medium for liberation from evil" (Cottom 37) and aligns its

force with feminist aspirations. When Ellena Rosalba, who is imprisoned in a convent in *The Italian*, discovers a window from which she can see mountain cliffs, ancient trees, and thunderous waterfalls, she finds that

> the consciousness of her prison was lost, while her eyes ranged over the wide and freely-sublime scene without. . . . With a mind thus elevated, how insignificant would appear to her the transactions, and the sufferings of this world! How poor the boasted power of man, when the fall of a single cliff from these mountains would with ease destroy thousands of his race assembled on the plains below! How would it avail them, that they were accoutred for battle, armed with all the instruments of destruction that human invention ever fashioned? Thus man, the giant who now held her in captivity, would shrink to the diminutiveness of a fairy; and she would experience, that his utmost force was unable to enchain her soul, or compel her to fear him, while he was destitute of virtue. (90–91)

In this passage, "man, the giant" who holds Ellena "in captivity" is not an individual tyrant but an entire system. By contemplating the power of nature, Radcliffe's heroines are inspired to dream revolutionary dreams, to envision a force capable of destroying the "power of man." In the process, they are emotionally reconstituted and empowered, saying to themselves: "If I am condemned to misery, surely I could endure it with more fortitude in scenes like these [mountains], than amidst the tamer landscapes of nature! Here, the objects seem to impart somewhat of their own force, their own sublimity, to the soul" (*The Italian* 62–63). For Radcliffe's heroines the contemplation of sublime nature is an essential, soul-renewing pleasure.

In *Frankenstein*, Mary Shelley explicitly associates her creature with the sublime. His physical stature is huge and rugged, like Burke's sublime, and his emotional energy is titanic. Throughout the novel, the sublime Alpine mountains and Arctic wastelands provide a cosmic reflection of the creature's inner desolation. Like Radcliffe's sublime, however, Shelley's creature is aligned not with masculine power but rather with natural forces that frustrate masculine ambition. He is the "other," a mysterious entity who has no place in the patriarchal order and who represents the frightening sexuality that could destroy the father's world. Symbolically, the "monster" constructed by Frankenstein is the same creature as the "woman" constructed by patriarchy. Frankenstein thinks the creature is beautiful until it comes to life; then he heaps on it all the contempt that Burke suggests is masked by "love." Shelley is not only commenting on Burke and rewriting Milton's *Paradise Lost*; she is also responding to the ancient tradition of Greek and Christian philosophy that transformed women into monsters. In the fourth century Chrysostom called the ordinary woman a "'necessary evil, a natural temptation, a desirable calamity, a domestic peril, a deadly fascination and a painted ill.' Aquinas said that woman could legitimately be considered 'defective and misbegotten.' . . . And in a sermon preached before Elizabeth, Bishop John Aylmer described woman as 'in every way doltified with the dregs of the devil's dunghill'" (Sekora, *Luxury* 59).[7] The patristic descriptions are strikingly similar to the terms used by hostile characters in *Frankenstein* to describe the creature. Mary Shelley responds to this vilification by suggesting that patriarchs will be destroyed by the monsters they create. Not only does Frankenstein lose his family and his life, but before he can die he is reduced to infantile dependence on the creature to whom he denied nurturance. He is forced to eat the food and wear the clothes his creature prepares for him during their ritualistic pursuit of each other over the Arctic wildernesses. As fittingly punished as Frankenstein, Walton becomes deadlocked in the Arctic seas he has attempted to penetrate.

Like her Gothic predecessors, Charlotte Brontë sometimes depicts nature as a powerful female force—a place of maternal refuge. Near despair after learning about Rochester's secret plan to commit bigamy, Jane Eyre is saved by a dream of a female moon that whispers to her spirit, "My daughter, flee temptation." Jane replies, "Mother, I will" (346). Brontë replaces Father God with Mother Nature, and Jane's connection with this natural force enables her to escape from Rochester's unfair designs upon her. As Jane says, "Nature seemed to me benign and good; I thought she loved me, outcast as I was; and I, who from man could anticipate only mistrust, rejection, insult, clung to her with filial fondness. To-night, at least, I would be her guest, as I was her child; my mother would lodge me without money and without price" (350). In this time of crisis, Jane spends a comforting night "nestled to the breast of the hill" (351).

Mother Nature, however, does not remain a safe haven for Jane. The next morning, she discovers "Want," by which she means not only hunger and thirst but also "a human being's wants" for human community—something "nature" cannot provide (351). As Margaret Homans has shown, Jane grows to understand that a permanent identification of herself with nature would be fatal (97). The "night-wind" and the "still frost" lead her to contemplate "the friendly numbness of death," whereas a dim light glimmering in a window—a sign of human society—draws her towards life. Thus Brontë suggests that although nature may provide temporary refuge from evil, it cannot solve human problems. Society is necessary for Jane's long-term survival.

In comparison to Gothic novels, slave narratives do not devote much space to describing an *idea* of nature; the authors were more concerned with survival in the material natural world. While authors of Gothic novels usually saw traveling as an exciting adventure in studying exotic places and peoples, fugitive slaves in antebellum America usually associated traveling with the experience of being enslaved or attempting to escape from slavery. Slave narrators also faced different generic constraints than Gothic novelists. The white abolitionists who sponsored slave narratives expected short, "objective" accounts of the evils of slavery; therefore, the authors of slave narratives could not indulge in the long Romantic descriptions of nature that characterize Radcliffian Gothic. Nonetheless, there are some similarities in the ways that "nature" functions in both genres.

Slave narratives attack the patriarchal association of slaves with brute nature by emphasizing the humanity of black people and the brutality of slaveholders. In slave narratives, as in Gothic novels, evil and good derive from human beings. Nature is morally neutral, and its neutrality makes it both a potential refuge from human evil and a potential source of physical hardship. Like Jane Eyre, protagonists in slave narratives flee into nature to escape from oppression, but in time nature proves inhospitable and the protagonists must find a human community in order to survive.

In her narrative, Nancy Prince describes the ocean as a potential refuge from slave traders. She recounts the story of her stepfather, who was captured by slave traders in Africa but escaped from a slave ship by jumping overboard with a friend and swimming to the shore of a free state. He repeatedly tells his children about "the beautiful moon-lit night when they two launched their bodies into the deep, for liberty" (6). Nature provides a route to freedom, but it is a fundamentally indifferent, often dangerous reality. When the two men attempt to swim ashore, "their feet were pricked with a sea-plant that grew under water [and] they had to retreat" until they could find a safe spot (6). Despite the dangers, many slaves seek refuge from slavery in the sea; indeed, Prince's stepfather explains that "no search was made for us; it was supposed we were drowned, as many had jumped over-board on the voyage" (7).

For fugitive slaves in the Caribbean and Latin America, wilderness areas that Radcliffe would have described as sublime were important primarily because of their inaccessibility to slaveholders. Many maroons found refuge in mountainous and desolate areas that were too rugged for white armies to control. The islands and coastal areas that could be controlled and cultivated were never the "paradise" that is marketed for twentieth-century tourists; they were sites of torture and death for millions of slaves. Mary Prince describes typical work in the West Indies, where slaves "worked through the heat of the day; the sun flaming upon our heads like fire, and raising salt blisters in those parts which were not completely covered. Our feet and legs, from standing in the salt water for so many hours, soon became full of dreadful boils, which eat down in some cases to the very bone, afflicting the sufferers with great torment" (10). Under conditions like this, the death rate of slaves was alarmingly high, much higher than that of slaves in the United States.[8]

Perhaps Harriet Jacobs most aptly dramatizes the role of "nature" in the lives of slaves when she describes hiding in Snaky Swamp as part of her desperate attempt to escape from Dr. Flint. Snaky Swamp is a terrifying place—hot, dark, and filled with mosquitoes and poisonous snakes. Jacobs recalls that "I dreaded to enter this hiding-place. But I was in no situation to choose" (112). After one night, she is covered with mosquito bites and running "a burning fever" (113). Nonetheless, she concludes that "even those large, venomous snakes were less dreadful to my imagination than the white men in that community called civilized" (113).

RECONSTRUCTING CHILDHOOD

In a 1985 conversation with Gloria Naylor, Toni Morrison said, "I used to live in this world, I mean really lived in it. I knew it. I used to belong here. And at some point I didn't belong anymore. I was somebody's parent, somebody's this, somebody's that, but there was no me in this world. And I was looking for that dead girl" ("A Conversation" 590). Her search for the "dead girl" she had once been—or fantasized—led her, among other things, to study narratives of slavery and to write *Beloved*. Struggling to escape from patriarchal strictures and to "really live" in their worlds, the protagonists of Gothic novels and slave narratives try to imagine a time before patriarchal ideology colonized their bodies and minds. Often the texts construct the protagonist's childhood as a time of "real life" and freedom. By reconstructing child-hood, the authors attempt to resurrect a "dead girl"—a self who has been written out of the social order. The danger of this reconstruction is that sometimes the authors idealize childhood in a way that sup-ports the father's order. However, the goal of this reconstruction is to find a free self, a child who represents the possibilities of life beyond patriarchy. Like Alice Miller, many nineteenth-century women writers yearned for a day when they could view children—and their child-hood selves—"as messengers from a world we once deeply knew, but which we have long since forgotten, who can reveal to us more about the true secrets of life, and also our own lives, than our parents ever were able to" (xi).

Ann Radcliffe, like Wordsworth, idealizes childhood as a prelap-sarian time during which the child lives happily in an Edenic garden with her father and mother. However, as I discussed in chapter 2, her texts subtly but persistently suggest that this idyllic home is a dan-gerous mirage. Writing sixty years later, Charlotte Brontë explicitly broke literary conventions by representing Jane Eyre's childhood as a torturous period of isolation, terror, and confinement. Twice before crises in the novel, Jane dreams about an infant. After her first series of dreams, she learns that John Reed, her childhood tormentor, has committed suicide. After her second series of dreams, her wedding is disrupted by the news that Rochester already has a wife. Both events are shocking and painful to Jane, but they also liberate her from male tyrants and from her false mother, Mrs. Reed. Thus liberated, Jane can be reborn and nurtured in the arms of mother nature. In the only dream she describes in detail, Jane is "burdened with the charge of a little child: a very small creature, too young and feeble to walk, and which shivered in [her] cold arms, and wailed piteously in [her] ear" (309). This feeble infant represents the repressed girl within Jane who needs to be nurtured back to life.

In *Wuthering Heights*, Emily Brontë associates the freedom of Catherine and Heathcliff's childhood with the sublime power of na-ture. When Catherine is dying—stifled by the hypocritical savagery of society—she remembers her wild childhood days with Heathcliff on the moors. Trapped in her room in society, buried in her enforced femininity and false identity, she longs for her childhood self. She cries, "Oh, I'm burning! I wish I were out of doors! I wish I were a girl again, half savage and hardy, and free . . . and laughing at injuries, not maddening under them! Why am I so changed? why does my blood rush into a hell of a tumult at a few words? I'm sure I should be myself were I once among the heather on those hills" (163). For Emily Brontë, as for most female Gothic novelists and slave narrators, the reconstructed childhood self is not subject to the Law of the Father (Homans 118).

Authors of both genres repeatedly depict their childhood selves as much freer to imagine an "agreeable" world than their adult selves. In her introduction to *Frankenstein*, Mary Shelley recalls that she loved to write as a child, but "I had a dearer pleasure than this, which was the formation of castles in the air—the indulging in waking dreams. . . . My dreams were at once more fantastic and agreeable than my writings. In the latter I was a close imitator—rather doing as others had done than putting down the suggestions of my own mind. What I wrote was intended at least for one other eye—my childhood's companion and friend; but my dreams were all my own; I accounted for them to nobody; they were my refuge when annoyed—my dearest pleasure when free" (51). Despite his progressive neglect of her, the favorite "companion and friend" to whom Shelley refers here was her father. Thus this passage suggests that the young Mary Wollstonecraft Godwin was always aware at some level of the inhibiting force of her father's gaze. When she assumed the role of writer, she was compelled to imitate, to use a language that was not her own. In her search for a creative space that is her own, she imagines her childhood as a time when she still owned her dreams, and they were "fantastic and agreeable." She recognizes that as an adult even her dreams are colonized—and they have turned monstrous.

In her most famous dream, the first sight that frightens her is "the pale student of unhallowed arts kneeling beside the thing he had put together" (*Frankenstein* 55). Then she sees the "hideous" creature this man has made, and "frightful must it be," this creature who, like Shelley herself, was constructed in man's image (55). Unlike most Gothic protagonists, Frankenstein's creature is deprived of even the illusion of childhood happiness; he was created as an adult and abandoned immediately. His only moments of happiness in the novel occur when he watches the De Lacey family; their idyllic family life creates for him a vision of what he desires.

Like Emily Brontë, Jane Austen in *Northanger Abbey* represents Catherine's childhood as a happy time free from the restrictions of femininity. As the famous first lines of Austen's novel state, "No one who had ever seen Catherine Morland in her infancy, would have supposed her born to be a heroine. . . . She was fond of all boys' plays. . . . She was moreover noisy and wild, hated confinement and cleanliness, and loved nothing so well in the world as rolling down the green slope at the back of the house" (37–38). In order to survive in the adult world, Catherine must learn to be quiet and submissive instead of "noisy and wild"; she must learn to value restrictive feminine clothes, to preserve her clean whiteness, and to suppress her love for adventure and action.

In most Gothic novels memories of childhood are mixed with pain because the protagonists have, in varying degrees, experienced emotional deprivation in childhood. Nonetheless, they yearn to recover the self-assertion and resilience they had as children or, in the case of Frankenstein's creature, the youthful hope that they would someday find happiness by becoming part of a loving human community. Growing into adulthood, they discover instead that their initiation into patriarchal capitalistic society means self-alienation and isolation.

For the female slaves represented in the narratives, childhood ends more abruptly and more painfully than for Gothic heroines. Enslaved girls fall from (at best) a very short period of childhood happiness into a realization of the brutal realities of a racist slave society. Nonetheless, the exceptional slave women who survived to write their narratives frequently recalled happy days of childhood innocence—a time before they knew they were enslaved. For Harriet Jacobs, memories of her childhood, especially "tender memories of my good old grandmother," are "like light, fleecy clouds floating over a dark and troubled sea" (201). This image concludes her narrative, bringing her readers back to her opening sentence: "I was born a slave; but I never knew it till six years of happy childhood had passed away" (5). Throughout her narrative, Jacobs represents memories of childhood days shared with beloved family members as a major source of her psychological strength.

However, the slave narrators' adult perspectives often render their memories of childhood bittersweet. When Jacobs remembers the happy days of childhood, she is forced to recollect as well the many betrayals and disappointments that her parents endured at the hands of slaveholders and their untimely deaths when she was still a young child. Ambivalence is also evident in Mary Prince's recollection of the time she spent in childhood with the daughter of a beloved mistress: "I was made quite a pet of by Miss Betsey, and loved her very much. She used to lead me about by the hand, and call me her little nigger. This was the happiest period of my life; for I was too young to understand rightly my condition as a slave" (1). Prince's mature understanding of the demeaning nature of Miss Betsey's attitude is clearly expressed in this passage. Prince's tone is bitterly ironic; she realizes that her childhood innocence allowed her to enjoy an illusion of happiness—and that illusion was happier than anything else she would find in a racist, patriarchal slave culture.

Although the authors of slave narratives and Gothic novels simultaneously create and subvert idyllic recollections of childhood, their writing attempts to rescue a dead self "from the grave of time and inattention. Her fingernails maybe in the first book; face and legs, perhaps, the second time. Little by little bringing her back into living life" (Morrison, "A Conversation" 593). In moments of epiphany, readers may catch glimpses of her.

WOMEN WRITERS between 1790 and 1865 did not, in their Gothic fiction or in their autobiographical narratives, imagine futuristic feminist utopias or evoke Amazonian prehistories. Rather, their texts contain only brief moments of escape from the historical realities of American slavery and the Gothic nightmares that symbolically represent the male-dominated world of the late eighteenth and early nineteenth centuries. As the feminist philosopher Alison Jaggar has stated, in the historical world "freedom is a social achievement and [it] cannot be achieved by isolated individuals in the absence of a general reordering of society" (306). As long as women in general are oppressed, no woman is free.

Eighteenth- and nineteenth-century writers of Gothic novels and slave narratives expressed ambivalent feelings about the possibilities of social reform. Some of them not only wrote about the need for liberation but also fought for enfranchisement, access to education, and improved economic opportunities. For example, in addition to claiming power over language, "Old Elizabeth" established "a school for coloured orphans" in Michigan (19). For Elizabeth, as for Charlotte Brontë (who dreamed of establishing a school for girls) and her characters Jane Eyre and Lucy Snowe (who succeed), establishing a school for disempowered members of society was both an act of social justice and a creative way to heal childhood feelings of isolation and abandonment.

Some British women, including Charlotte Brontë's friend Mary Taylor, attempted to escape from economic oppression by emigrating to less "civilized" places like New Zealand and Australia. Taylor urged women "that they need only just move to send the horror [of economic injustice against women] away. . . . The new world will be no Paradise but still much better than the nightmare" of not being able to earn "enough to live by" in England.[9] Ironically, many escaped American slaves (like the Crafts) fled to England to escape from the miserable economic conditions created by American racism. As it turned out, neither emigrating from nor immigrating to England provided a long-term solution to gender- and race-based economic oppression. Mary Taylor eventually returned to England where she wrote essays and a novel describing the importance of paid work for women (Peters 411–12). Escaped slaves living in England often longed to reunite with family and friends living in America, and they continued their abolitionist agitation as well as they could from across the seas.

While yearning and fighting for freedom, female writers of Gothic novels and slave narratives always return to the realities of constriction and deprivation that characterize life for women in a patriarchal culture. The word "escape" may give them "a quicker blood / A sudden expectation / A flying attitude!" but ultimately their texts echo Emily Dickinson's predicament: "I tug childish at my bars / Only to fail again!" Nonetheless, eighteenth- and nineteenth-century women writers fought valiantly for liberation, and they won important local battles—or at least temporary respite. Their writing affirms Audre Lorde's assertion that women are not only casualties—we are also warriors.

CONCLUSION

PROBLEMS
OF
CLOSURE

The thing that irks me most is this shattered prison, after all. I'm tired, tired of being enclosed here. I'm wearying to escape into that glorious world, and to be always there: not seeing it dimly through tears, and yearning for it through the walls of an aching heart, but really with it, and in it.

Emily Brontë, *Wuthering Heights*

Reader, my story ends with freedom; not in the usual way, with marriage. I and my children are now free! We are as free from the power of slaveholders as are the white people of the north; and though that, according to my ideas, is not saying a great deal, it is a vast improvement in *my* condition. The dream of my life is not yet realized.

Harriet Jacobs, *Incidents in the Life of a Slave Girl*

EVERY GOTHIC NOVEL and every slave narrative written by a woman attests to her longing for freedom. The texts represent protagonists who, against tremendous odds, fight against subjugation and win many battles. However, as the above quotations suggest, triumphs are only partial and transient. Moments of escape from the horrors of patriarchal domination provide the heroines of Gothic novels and slave narratives with essential periods of respite from pain. If escape were complete and enduring, it would provide satisfying closure for the texts. However, because the authors insist that escape is transitory at best, the problem of how to end the narratives, how to get heroines out of their labyrinths of terror, becomes a major issue.

Female Gothic novelists deal with the problem of closure in a variety of illuminating ways. Writers like Ann Radcliffe and Jane Austen, who were fairly conservative compared to Wollstonecraft, Shelley, and the Brontës, subtly rebelled against conventional closure. Their overly tidy conclusions draw attention to their own artifice, as the narrator notes with self-reflexive humor at the end of *Northanger Abbey*: "My readers . . . will see in the tell-tale compression of the pages before them, that we are all hastening together to perfect felicity" (246). According to the conventions of the novel, "perfect felicity" means that the heroine marries the hero at the end of the story. However, since the novels of Radcliffe and Austen have all along exposed the tyranny institutionalized in marriage, they have undercut at least that prospect of a happy resolution.

In a bolder, more direct style, Mary Wollstonecraft concludes her first novel (*Mary, A Fiction*) with an explicit reversal of the traditional happy ending. Instead of celebrating a marriage, Wollstonecraft's heroine envisions a day when marriage will be abolished. The last sentence of the novel states, "In moments of solitary sadness, a gleam of joy would dart across [Mary's] mind—She thought she was hastening to that world *where there is neither marrying*, nor giving in marriage" (68).[1] The lack of conclusion to Wollstonecraft's second novel, *Maria; or, The Wrongs of Woman*, is emblematic of the difficulties closure posed for female Gothic novelists. Wollstonecraft drafted segments of three concluding chapters which extend the novel's bleak analysis of the ways in which society oppresses women. In the last fragmented pages, Maria goes to court to defend her lover Darnford against her husband's charges that Darnford was guilty of seduction and adultery. She speaks eloquently about her husband's cruelty and the integrity of freely chosen adult love, concluding, "I claim then a divorce" (198). However, the judge rules that "if women were allowed to plead their feelings, as an excuse or palliation of infidelity, it was opening a floodgate for immorality. What virtuous woman thought of her feelings?" (199). He continues that, if her husband imprisoned her in a madhouse, he was justified in so doing because "indeed the conduct of the lady did not appear that of a person of sane mind" (199).[2]

Clearly Wollstonecraft intended to conclude her novel with an attack on the injustice of patriarchal law, particularly marriage laws. At the same time, she wanted to leave Maria with some amount of personal happiness in her socially subversive relationship with Darnford. Ultimately Wollstonecraft was unable to envision a genuinely satisfying heterosexual relationship; every attempt to describe Maria and Darnford's union is filled with contradictions: "With Darnford [Maria] did not taste uninterrupted felicity; there was a volatility in his manner which often distressed her; but love gladdened the scene; besides, he was the most tender, sympathizing creature in the world. A fondness for the sex often gives an appearance of humanity to the behaviour of men, who have small pretensions to the reality; and they seem to love others, when they are only pursuing their own gratification" (192). The narrator appears confused and indecisive, leaving the reader full of doubt about Darnford's "love" and "tenderness." Despite her passionate defense of women's right to love, Wollstonecraft's writing constantly expresses skepticism about the possibility of egalitarian heterosexual relationships.

Wollstonecraft, then, had difficulty closing *The Wrongs of Woman* because she did not want to end in despair but wanted to be truthful to her own experience of the world. We will never know how she would have resolved her conflicting ideas for the novel's conclusion because a male doctor intervened and ended her life. At the age of thirty-eight, Wollstonecraft

> was in excellent health and had three years earlier borne without complications a first daughter. . . . She chose to give birth to this second baby at home, attended only by a midwife, Mrs. Blenkinsop. But when Mary Wollstonecraft failed to expel the placenta, Mrs. Blenkinsop hastily summoned Doctor Poignard who, without washing his hands . . . , pulled out the fragmented placenta piece by piece. In the process, he introduced the infection of the uterus that ten days later killed Mary Wollstonecraft Godwin. (Mellor 1)

This conclusion to Wollstonecraft's life and to her last novel is a fitting symbol of the difficulties of creativity for women in a male-dominated world.

Wollstonecraft left behind a dual legacy of inestimable value to the future of feminism: her writing and her daughter, Mary Wollstonecraft Shelley. At the same time, her conclusion was doubly tragic. Her writing was unfinished, her daughter was motherless, and both were subjected to decades of abuse that Wollstonecraft perhaps could have deflected had she lived. As Mellor observes:

> The widespread denunciation of Mary Wollstonecraft as a revolutionary, atheist, and whore after the publication of Godwin's ill-judged *Memoirs* made it socially impossible for a respectable, educated woman of the early nineteenth century to advocate Wollstonecraft's lifestyle or to celebrate her as a leader of the women's movement. More personally, it eroded Mary Shelley's belief that her mother's life and career provided a viable alternative social role for women. The absence from [Mary Shelley's] novels of independent, self-fulfilled, nurturant women records Mary Shelley's oblique recognition that such women could not survive in the world she knew. (210)

The abuse inflicted upon Wollstonecraft for her intellectual courage and emotional and sexual honesty warned future generations of
women writers to silence or disguise their social criticism.

Writing fifty years after Wollstonecraft, Emily Brontë was another
extraordinarily courageous and uncompromising thinker who had no
patience with social conventions. Whereas Wollstonecraft flaunted conventions in hopes of changing society, Brontë wholeheartedly rejected
society. In the world of *Wuthering Heights*, attempts at social reform
would be laughable; rebels against the culturally imposed masculine-
feminine dichotomy and the classist social structure can survive only
outside the material world, as ghostly ideals haunting our consciousness. Catherine and Heathcliff's attempts to negotiate life inside the
patriarchal order are not only unsuccessful but are ultimately self-
diminishing.

Emily Brontë's skepticism about material reality is matched by Mary
Shelley's despair about human society; however, other female Gothic
novelists hoped to find a viable life in this world. Charlotte Brontë
tried to escape despair by refusing to think about the fundamental
injustices built into the social superstructure. She explained to her
friend Elizabeth Gaskell that "certainly there are evils which our own
best efforts will reach; but as certainly there are other evils—deep-
rooted in the foundations of the social system—which no efforts of
ours can touch: of which we cannot complain; of which it is advisable
not too often to think" (Gaskell 422). Avoiding her sister's skepticism,
Charlotte focused her attention on specific social injustices, such as
women's lack of educational and economic opportunities. She also insisted on woman's right to act as a desiring subject. In this political-
sexual agenda, she followed in the footsteps of Mary Wollstonecraft.

However, the conclusions of Charlotte Brontë's novels, like the conclusions of Wollstonecraft's novels, indicate her growing sense of the
impossibility of women and men being able to escape the socially imposed sado-masochistic sexual dynamic. Even in her first published
novel, *Jane Eyre*, Brontë could not create a happy ending without
heavy-handed authorial intrusion in the guise of supernatural inter-
vention (Jane and Rochester hearing each other's voices over many
miles). And even in this fairy-tale ending, Rochester must be blinded
and maimed to ensure that he will not attempt to reassert dominance
over Jane. In her later industrial novel, *Shirley*, Brontë could imagine
no escape from violent sexual politics (which, significantly, she con-
nects to violent class conflicts). Louis and Shirley's disturbing union at

the end of the novel reveals Brontë's profound doubts about hetero-sexual relationships in a patriarchal culture.

If Brontë's "real, cool, and solid" industrial novel ends bleakly (*Shirley* 40), her final Gothic novel, *Villette*, is even less hopeful. By the 1850s, Brontë could no longer bring herself to write a fairy-tale ending. Responding to her editor's and father's pleas for a happy conclusion to *Villette*, she added this paragraph near the end of the novel: "Leave sunny imaginations hope. Let it be theirs to conceive the delight of joy born again fresh out of great terror, the rapture of rescue from peril, the wondrous reprieve from dread, the fruition of return. Let them picture union and a happy succeeding life" (491). Brontë herself had seen too much of life to envision a magical resolution. While the novel's unsavory characters live long and prosperous lives, Lucy Snowe bleakly imagines storms and shipwrecks for herself and thousands of women like her, "a thousand weepers, praying in agony on waiting shores, listen[ing] for that voice, but it was not uttered" (491).

Although Mary Shelley and Emily Brontë were unable to imagine happy existences for their protagonists in the present world, they refused to kill all hope for the future. At the end of *Frankenstein*, Shelley's creature is "borne away by the waves and lost in darkness and distance," but he is still alive, which leaves us with a faint hope that at some future time he will find a voice and a place in the world (261). Similarly, in the deliberately mythic *Wuthering Heights*, Brontë leaves the ghosts of Catherine and Heathcliff in "unquiet slumbers." Their restless spiritual energy is the essence of life for Brontë, the soul of existence that she describes in her poem "No Coward Soul Is Mine" as the

> God within my breast
> Almighty ever present Deity
> Life, that in me has rest
> As I, Undying Life, have power in Thee.

At the end of *Wuthering Heights*, Lockwood may wonder "how anyone could ever imagine unquiet slumbers, for the sleepers in that quiet earth" (367), but for many readers, glimpses of the ghosts of Catherine and Heathcliff keep alive the hope that someday there will be "a glorious world . . . incomparably above and beyond" the familiar but frightening world of Lintons, Lockwoods, and Josephs, a world in which Catherine and Heathcliff could live (196–97).

TRADITIONALLY, comic fiction ends in marriage, and tragic fiction ends in death. Between 1790 and 1865 female Gothic novelists developed a genre that was neither comic nor tragic. They struggled to expose the terrors of life without conceding to despair; to attain that goal they needed to create a literary form for revolt rather than for the usual ends of comedy or tragedy. Because there is nothing revolutionary in a heroine's marriage or in her death, female Gothic novels conclude tensely, refusing to affirm either hope or despair.

Female slave narratives maintain a similar tension, but the authors faced different problems. Unlike the English novel, the American slave narrative is inherently revolutionary. African American writers had both to employ and to subvert a revolutionary discourse that was dominated by whites and thus limited in its vision. White sponsorship of black writing often meant white co-option. Most American slave narratives were framed by white-authored texts, a fitting symbol of how blacks were held captive even in the "free" North. Furthermore, in many narratives, such as Louisa Picquet's, it is "not black recollection, but white interrogation [that] brings order to the narration" (Sekora, "Black Message" 509). Picquet's rebellion is confined within the space allowed her by the Reverend H. Mattison; *he* provides the form— beginning, middle, and end.

Sekora notes that "in the [slave] narrative it is antislavery as a form that provides closure" ("Black Message" 502). Slave narratives typically end with a chapter entitled "Free at Last!" and with a call for the abolition of slavery. Mary Prince's narrative is representative; her concluding sentence exhorts her English readers to demand that "all the poor blacks be given free, and slavery done up for evermore" (23). White-dominated antislavery discourse left little space for "inquiry into a slave's life after slavery" (Sekora, "Black Message" 502). Jacobs's letters and Douglass's second autobiography reveal that white abolitionist leaders like Harriet Beecher Stowe and William Lloyd Garrison viewed black people's stories as raw resources for whites to plunder. White sponsors usually wanted to "compel a black author to approve, to authorize white institutional power. The black message will be sealed in a white envelope" (Sekora 502).

The ex-slave women who wrote narratives often escaped from the limitations of the white antislavery form by mixing genres in their texts. Nancy Prince evaded generic limitations by mixing the slave narrative genre with the popular nineteenth-century genre of the travel narrative. She entitled her text *A Narrative of the Life and Travels of*

Mrs. Nancy Prince and devoted as much space to describing the customs and fashions of foreign countries as to describing her struggles against slavery and racism. However, this combination is not very effective; her social analyses are occasionally profound but scattered and underdeveloped, and her story is difficult to follow. She concludes with several pages of pieties in which she represents herself as a pilgrim who has been "purified through fire" and has accepted her sufferings "meekly" (88). The *Memoir of Old Elizabeth* is a more successful mixture of genres. By combining a slave narrative with a religious narrative, Elizabeth was able to devote most of her text to describing her struggles against racism and sexism *after* manumission. The religious framework also enabled her to claim divine justification for her radical activism as a black female preacher in the face of human opposition.

By integrating the revolutionary language of the slave narrative tradition with the feminist potential of nineteenth-century women's sentimental fiction, Harriet Jacobs was able to write a uniquely insightful book—the masterpiece of the female slave narrative tradition and a Gothic metatext. Yet even Jacobs's accomplishment was lessened by the expectations of white abolitionists. Jacobs's editor, Lydia Maria Child, was a sensitive feminist-abolitionist and an unusually benign white editor of black texts. She nonetheless believed that she knew best what form Harriet Jacobs's story should take. After reading Jacobs's manuscript, Child told Jacobs that she (Child) had "very little occasion to alter the language, which is wonderfully good, for one whose opportunities for education have been so limited. The events are interesting, and well told; the remarks are also good, and to the purpose" (Jacobs 244). However, Child continued, she had transposed "sentences and pages, so as to bring the story into continuous *order,* and the remarks into *appropriate* places. I think you will see that this renders the story much more clear and entertaining" (Jacobs 244, original emphasis). In particular, Child wanted to omit Jacobs's original conclusion, which described a slave revolt led by John Brown against the United States arsenal at Harpers Ferry, Virginia, in 1839. Thus instead of ending with a portrayal of black revolutionary action, Jacobs concludes her narrative with a chapter describing how a white woman bought her freedom.[3]

Like Charlotte Brontë, Jacobs was forced by her editor to alter her conclusion, but, again like Brontë, Jacobs managed to maintain subversive elements in her last chapter. She expresses outrage over the fact that in the end the Flint family received money for her, and she makes it clear that her life in the North is not really free. Jacobs did all she could as an individual to escape from slavery, but she recognizes that there are no individual solutions to systemic problems. In Margaret Fuller's words, "While any one is base, none can be entirely free and noble" (21). Jacobs and her family can only be as free as the rest of society, and Jacobs points out that that "is not saying a great deal" (201).

During the century after the Emancipation Proclamation, few white Americans wanted to question the meaning of "freedom" in the lives of black Americans. Unfortunately, African Americans found that "freedman status was not an end to the process of marginalization but merely the end of the beginning" (Patterson 249). What followed was "a new dialectic of domination and dependence" (294), a dialectic we do not yet fully understand. The women who wrote Gothic novels and slave narratives between 1790 and 1865 recognized that they were struggling for a type of liberation that they would never attain in their lifetimes. Their texts focus on the terrifying and often overwhelming forces of oppression in a racist, classist, patriarchal world. Nonetheless, the authors kept alive visions of a better world and celebrated moments of ecstasy in the present world, moments that are permeated with "the fragrance of freedom" (Jacobs 250). Since 1865 several generations of feminist and anti-racist writers have fought sexual/textual battles for liberation; many of them have drawn on the female Gothic and slave narrative traditions for inspiration.

NOTES

INTRODUCTION
WOMEN AND SLAVERY

1. Astell's feminist insights were weakened by her attempt to advocate women's rights while maintaining devout Christian views and "high Anglican and Tory sympathies" (Hill 2). This attempt entangled her in multiple contradictions because Biblical texts mandate a clear hierarchy: wives, children, and slaves are to obey the paterfamilias, and he in turn is to treat them kindly. See, for example, Eph. 5.22–6.9 and Col. 3.18–4.1. For an illuminating discussion of Astell's contradictory beliefs, see Rogers.

2. For an overview of laws from Aristotle to eighteenth-century England that restricted women's education, "walks, dress, food, drink, and holidays" as well as confiscated their economic resources, legislated their sexuality, and condemned them wholesale as a "necessary evil," see Sekora, *Luxury* 58–59.

3. A similar reversal is evident in rhetoric comparing workers and slaves. "Free" workers were originally compared to slaves by eighteenth-century proponents of slavery who scoffed at the idea of "freedom" and argued that slaves were better off than workers in England and the United States. Like feminists, labor reformers appropriated the masters' language and infused it with revolutionary meanings. For an extended analysis of the worker-slave analogy, see Gallagher 3–35.

4. Qtd. in Genovese 86. For a fuller discussion of slaveholders' patriarchal ideology, see Genovese 73–86.

5. Brantlinger breaks new ground by examining the influence of racist imperialism on British literature during the Victorian and Edwardian periods (1830–1914).

6. Genovese argues that between 1831 and 1861, "the condition of [American] slaves worsened with respect to access to freedom and the promise of eventual emancipation; it got better with respect to material conditions of life. . . . [The slaveholders'] position made perfect sense: Make the South safe for slaveholders by confirming the blacks in perpetual slavery and by making it possible for them to accept their fate" (51).

7. See Franklin 98–123.

8. See Daly, *Gyn/Ecology*. The forms of violence against women vary from

culture to culture. Not all women are victims of rape, battering, footbinding, genital mutilation, medical savagery, and witch-hunts, but all women are terrorized by the constant threat of violence.

9. Baym makes a similar point. She observes that women's texts repeatedly tell the same story, "in two parallel versions. In one, the heroine begins as a poor and friendless child. Most frequently an orphan, she sometimes only thinks herself to be one, or has by necessity been separated from her parents for an indefinite time. In the second, the heroine is a pampered heiress who becomes poor and friendless in midadolescence, through the death or financial failure of her legal protectors" (35). In both versions, the heroine is bereft of family.

10. See Rich, *Of Woman Born* 259.

11. Although slave narratives appealed to a popular audience, narratives written by men were much more widely distributed than narratives written by women. Some of the texts I discuss, such as Harriet Wilson's *Our Nig*, sold very few copies, for reasons examined in chapter 1.

12. I am, of course, using the term "feminist" anachronistically to describe political positions taken in support of justice for women. The term was coined in 1895.

CHAPTER ONE
BREAKING SILENCE

1. DeLamotte notes that Gothic fiction has always lent itself to definitions "by inventory" (4).

2. For an analysis of the ways Gothic fiction created the need for detective fiction, see Day 50–56.

3. Praz later revised his opinion of *Frankenstein*, if not of Mary Shelley's artistic abilities. In 1968 he wrote, "For the far-reaching implications of the main theme and for the grandiose scenery through which the mad chase takes place, Mrs. Shelley's novel ranks as the greatest achievement of the Gothic school, notwithstanding its frequent clichés of phrasing and situation and the occasionally disarming naivete" ("Introductory" 32).

4. For an insightful overview of criticism that discusses the subversive nature of Gothic literature, see Lovell 55–72. For a more general overview of Gothic criticism, see DeLamotte 3–15.

5. I am using the term "subject position" in a double sense, to refer to (a) the extent to which one is socially empowered as an agent of willful thought and action, and (b) the ways one is subject, both consciously and subconsciously, to a myriad of linguistic, psychological, political, and social forces. I am not suggesting that men are free agents of autonomous action, but that men and women are socially constructed as subjects in significantly different ways.

6. I am indebted to Toril Moi for the phrase "sexual/textual politics."

7. Sadleir was the first literary critic to identify one type of Gothic as "Radcliffian" and the other type as "Lewisite" (in 1929).

8. See McIntyre, Murray, Punter, and Ellis. In his biography of Radcliffe, Murray states that when "Radcliffe discovered the sensual subject matter in Matthew Lewis's *The Monk*—written in professed emulation of her *Udolpho*—she undertook to rub it out by (in effect) bowdlerizing the work in her next book, *The Italian*" (19). Murray posits a traditional opposition between women's (hypocritical) frigidity and men's (honest) sensuality. Belittling Radcliffe as a "prim moralist" whose texts contained "lily-white sensationalism" (19), he distorts the little he sees of Radcliffe's social critique.

9. I am using the concepts of the erotic and the pornographic as Griffin defines them in *Pornography and Silence*: "Pornography is an expression not of human erotic feeling and desire, and not of a love of the life of the body, but of a fear of bodily knowledge, and a desire to silence eros" (1).

10. Not a single one of Radcliffe's letters has survived. Murray points out that "the absolute lack of any correspondence from so easily a prolific writer as Mrs. Radcliffe is itself a curious anomaly in a time when the one legitimate literary expression allowed young ladies was the familiar exchange of thoughts provided by letter writing" (16).

11. For an analysis of Oedipal rebellions in Gothic novels by men, see Fiedler's *Love and Death in the American Novel* and Restuccia's insightful critique of Fiedler in "Female Gothic Writing."

12. Qtd. in Gilbert and Gubar 3.

13. See Russ, *How to Suppress Women's Writing*; Spencer, *The Rise of the Woman Novelist*; and Spender, *Mothers of the Novel*.

14. Coleridge, for example, "called the *Mysteries of Udolpho* 'the most interesting novel in the English language'" (Tompkins 250). Later in the century, Balzac "cited [Mary Shelley] and Ann Radcliffe as proof that women outdo men in imaginative invention" (Sunstein 366).

15. Morrison describes this form of torture in *Beloved* (71).

16. Of course even those slaves who did not read or write constantly produced subversive texts, in the forms of stories, songs, dances—multiple semiotic systems of protest. For a discussion of these texts, see Franklin.

17. For a more detailed discussion of Mattison's attitude towards Picquet and how slave narrators in general negotiated the temptation "to exploit the prurient appeal of their knowledge of patriarchalism's perversities," see Andrews, *To Tell* 242–47.

18. Adapted from Arthur Fauset's version of Truth's speech.

19. The continuing significance of Truth's question is suggested by the fact that at least two scholars have used it in the 1980s to title their books (Hooks, *Ain't I a Woman: Black Women and Feminism*, and White, *Ar'n't I a Woman? Female Slaves in the Plantation South*).

20. For an exploration of some of the troubles with Douglass's views on women and his place in the African American canon, see McDowell.

21. In June, shortly before Mary conceived "her hideous progeny," Byron recited *Christabel* and Percy "suddenly 'saw' Mary as the villainess with eyes for nipples . . . and ran screaming out of the room" (Sunstein 122). Polidori wrote a "terrible" story about "a skullheaded lady" who was gruesomely punished and murdered "for peeping through a key-hole" (seeking forbidden knowledge), as Mary recalled in her introduction to the 1831 edition of *Frankenstein* (ix). In her journal, Mary mentions hearing Lewis tell ghost stories at Byron's villa in August 1816 (57). She does not describe the stories, but she had read *The Monk* in 1814. She avoided Lewis's society in 1816.

Frankenstein's silenced creature not only represents Mary herself but also the baby she lost in March 1815. While Percy seemed cold and impatient with her grief, Mary continued to mourn. In a journal entry dated March 19, she wrote, "Dream that my little baby came to life again; that it had only been cold, and that we rubbed it before the fire, and it lived. Awake and find no baby. I think about the little thing all day. Not in good spirits" (*Journal* 41). In her novel, when the creature comes to life, the father runs away in horror.

CHAPTER TWO
LABYRINTHS OF TERROR

1. See Miller, *For Your Own Good: Hidden Cruelty in Child-Rearing and the Roots of Violence* and *Thou Shalt Not Be Aware: Society's Betrayal of the Child.*

2. I am indebted to John S. Wright for this observation.

3. For an analysis of the coercive aspects of heterosexuality in a patriarchal culture, see Rich, "Compulsory Heterosexuality and Lesbian Existence."

4. Terry Carr, an editor at Ace, interpreted the appeal of Ace's "long-selling and best-selling books" as follows: "The basic appeal . . . is to women who marry guys and then begin to discover that their husbands are strangers . . . so there's a simultaneous attraction/repulsion, love/fear going on. Most of the 'pure' Gothics tend to have a handsome, magnetic suitor or husband who may or may not be a lunatic and/or murderer" (qtd. in Russ, "Somebody's Trying to Kill Me" 32).

5. Like Emily, the narrator of Gilman's "The Yellow Wallpaper" begins her story tongue-in-cheek, wishing she could describe "a haunted house and reach the height of romantic felicity" (3). And, again like Emily, she soon stops laughing. She learns that in some terrifying ways her house *is* haunted.

6. Mellor points out that when "Frankenstein identifies Nature as female . . . he participates in a gendered construction of the universe whose ramifications are everywhere apparent in *Frankenstein*" ("Possessing Nature" 220). This sexual division renders him unable "to feel empathy for the creature" and "leads directly to his downfall" (221).

7. See also Gaskell 99–109.

8. For an analysis of Emily Brontë's detailed representation of English law, see Sanger.

9. Rich suggests that "profound skepticism, caution, and righteous paranoia about men may indeed be part of any healthy woman's response to the misogyny of male-dominated culture" ("Compulsory Heterosexuality" 65).

CHAPTER THREE
SISTERHOOD IN SLAVERY?

1. I am indebted to Michael Hancher for this insight.

2. Jacobs gives a particularly moving picture of a white mistress blaming her husband's victim: "I once saw a young slave girl dying soon after the birth of a child nearly white. In her agony she cried out, 'O Lord, come and take me!' Her mistress stood by, and mocked at her like an incarnate fiend. 'You suffer, do you?' she exclaimed. 'I am glad of it. You deserve it all, and more too.'" (13).

3. A slaveholding woman named Kate Stone who was opposed to slavery recorded in her diary, begun in 1861, that she visited, brought food to, and read to various slaves. She also mentions the death of "Jane Eyre, Malona's baby" (qtd. in Gwin 90). It is possible that Stone read *Jane Eyre* to slaves or discussed it with them.

4. For a thought-provoking analysis of Bertha Mason and imperialism in *Jane Eyre*, *Wide Sargasso Sea*, and *Frankenstein*, see Spivak. Also see responses to Spivak and further examinations of colonialism in *Jane Eyre* in Boumelha, Donaldson, Meyer, and Retan 211–22.

5. For another interesting reading of Linda Brent's nocturnal ordeals with Mrs. Flint, see Spillers 76–77.

6. Charlotte Brontë to William Smith Williams, April 12, 1850. Wise and Symington 3: 98–99.

7. According to Cora Kaplan, Mary Wollstonecraft, influenced by Jean-Jacques Rousseau, "first offered women this fateful choice between the opposed and moralized bastions of reason and feeling, which continues to determine much feminist thinking" (155).

8. Sedgwick argues that the fear of being buried alive is central to the Gothic genre. I see significant differences in how men and women represent live burials. Male Gothic novelists often bury heroines alive and then experiment with variations of torture. Lewis's Antonia is raped and murdered in a tomb; his Agnes is starved, tormented and nearly killed but miraculously and completely recovers from her entombment. Poe's Ligeia and Lady Madeline refuse to stay dead. Jacobs's experiences fit into a distinctly *female* Gothic pattern; she describes her pain without eroticizing or mystifying it. (Her legs and various muscles are permanently damaged from her seven-years' imprison-

ment.) Rather than simply being victimized, Jacobs chooses her "enclosure . . . to redirect her own and her children's destiny" (V. Smith 30).

9. Qtd. in Sterling 114.

10. See Rogers 71–81.

CHAPTER FOUR
MOMENTS OF ESCAPE

1. 329. White cites similar patterns of female resistance to slavery in the American South (70–90).

2. According to Patterson, "In order that the slave masters of the Americas might acquire 11 to 12 million slaves, at least 24 million persons were originally enslaved in Africa" (164).

3. Elizabeth describes several occasions where her verbal skill transforms an enemy into a friend. One time, a watchman tried to break up her meeting with "a few coloured sisters," but after Elizabeth said "a few words" to him, he turned "pale and trembled, and begged my pardon, . . . and wished us success" (11–12). Another time when Elizabeth is preaching, a white critic, "a great scripturian, fixed himself behind the door with pen and ink, in order to take down the discourse in short-hand; but the Almighty Being anointed me with such a portion of his Spirit, that he cast away his paper and pen, and heard the discourse with patience, and was much affected, for the Lord wrought powerfully on his heart. After meeting, he came forward and offered me his hand" (16).

4. For a different but insightful reading of the idea that a heroine is protected by her sense of "conscious worth," see DeLamotte 32–35.

5. Freedom and literacy are intimately linked in African American experience; indeed, Stepto asserts that the "primary pregeneric myth" that shapes the African American literary canon is "the quest for freedom and literacy" (ix).

6. But Radcliffe highlights the sinister side of this exchange, registering the father's subconscious resentment against the man who steals his daughter's affections in an incident in which St. Aubert, mistaking Valancourt for a bandit, shoots and wounds him.

7. For further analyses of parallels between the creature and "woman," see Hirsch, Tillotson, and Gilbert and Gubar.

8. Of the estimated 11 or 12 million Africans imported to the New World, 40 percent were brought to the Caribbean (Patterson 161). The death rate was so high that constant fresh imports were needed to replenish the enslaved labor force.

9. Taylor to Ellen Nussey, 9 Feb. 1849. Qtd. in Peters 280.

CONCLUSION
PROBLEMS OF CLOSURE

1. Ironically, Wollstonecraft is using a "sacred" text to advance her critique of a "sacred" institution. (Matt. 22.30: "For in the resurrection they neither marry, nor are given in marriage, but are as the angels of God in heaven.")

2. The judge's declaration that Maria is insane because she "thought of her feelings" and resisted her husband's will brings to mind the legal situation of slaves in America. Sekora and Baker point out that "between 1619 and 1776 colonial American law declared unruly or rebellious slaves to be, by definition, 'insane.' 'Slave insanity' became an omnibus legal category allowing slaveholders to punish without limit" (43).

3. Mrs. Bruce bought Jacobs's freedom from the Flints in opposition to Jacobs's will. Jacobs expressed her anger and disappointment in a letter to Amy Post: "I thank you for your kind expressions in regard to my freedom; but the freedom I had before the money was paid was dearer to me. God gave me *that* freedom; but man put God's image in the scales with the paltry sum of three hundred dollars. I served for my liberty as faithfully as Jacob served for Rachel. At the end, he had large possessions; but I was robbed of my victory; I was obliged to resign my crown, to rid myself of a tyrant" (Jacobs 204).

WORKS CITED

Abrams, M. H. *Natural Supernaturalism: Tradition and Revolution in Romantic Literature*. 1971. New York: Norton, 1973.

Andrews, William L. Introduction. *My Bondage and My Freedom*. By Frederick Douglass. Urbana: U of Illinois P, 1987.

———. *To Tell a Free Story: The First Century of Afro-American Autobiography, 1760–1865*. Urbana: U of Illinois P, 1986.

Aristotle. *Politics. Greek and Roman Slavery*. Ed. and trans. Thomas Weidemann. Baltimore: Johns Hopkins UP, 1981. 18–19.

Astell, Mary. *Reflections upon Marriage and Other Writings*. Ed. Bridget Hill. New York: St. Martin's, 1986.

Austen, Jane. *Northanger Abbey*. 1818. New York: Penguin, 1972.

Bakhtin, M. M. *The Dialogic Imagination: Four Essays*. Trans. Caryl Emerson and Michael Holquist. Austin: U of Texas P, 1981.

Banton, Michael. "Of Inhuman Bondage." Rev. of *Slavery and Social Death* by Orlando Patterson. *Times Literary Supplement* 9 Sept. 1983: 947–48.

Barthelemy, Anthony G. Introduction. *Collected Black Women's Narratives*. New York: Oxford, 1988. xxix–xlviii.

Barthes, Roland. *Mythologies*. New York: Hill, 1972.

Bayer-Berenbaum, Linda. *The Gothic Imagination: Expansion in Gothic Literature and Art*. London: Associated University Presses, 1982.

Baym, Nina. *Woman's Fiction: A Guide to Novels By and About Women in America, 1820–1870*. Ithaca: Cornell UP, 1978.

Beckford, William. *Vathek*. 1786. New York: Penguin, 1968.

Benjamin, Jessica. *The Bonds of Love: Psychoanalysis, Feminism, and the Problem of Domination*. New York: Pantheon, 1988.

Blount, Marcellus. "Southern Exposure: Women in a House Divided." Rev. of *Within the Plantation Household*, by Elizabeth Fox-Genovese. *Village Voice Literary Supplement* May 1989: 29.

Boumelha, Penny. "'And What Do the Women Do?': Jane Eyre, Jamaica and the Gentleman's House." *Southern Review* 21 (1988): 111–22.

Brantlinger, Patrick. *Rule of Darkness: British Literature and Imperialism, 1830–1914*. Ithaca: Cornell UP, 1988.

Braxton, Joanne M. *Black Women Writing Autobiography: A Tradition Within a Tradition*. Philadelphia: Temple UP, 1989.

Brontë, Anne. *The Tenant of Wildfell Hall*. 1848. New York: Penguin, 1979.

Brontë, Anne, Charlotte, Branwell, and Emily. *Selected Brontë Poems*. Ed. Edward Chitham and Tom Winnifrith. Oxford: Blackwell, 1985.

Brontë, Charlotte. *Jane Eyre*. 1847. New York: Penguin, 1986.

———. *Shirley*. 1849. New York: Penguin, 1974.

———. *Villette*. 1853. London: Dent, 1983.

Brontë, Emily. *Wuthering Heights*. 1847. New York: Penguin, 1985.

Brown, Charles Brockden. *Wieland; or, The Transformation*. 1798. New York: Dolphin, 1962.

Brown, William Wells. *Narrative of William W. Brown, A Fugitive Slave, Written By Himself*. 1847. *Puttin' on Ole Massa*. Ed. Gilbert Osofsky. New York: Harper, 1969. 173–223.

Burke, Edmund. *A Philosophical Enquiry into the Origin of Our Ideas of the Sublime and Beautiful*. 1759. Notre Dame: U of Notre Dame P, 1968.

Carby, Hazel V. *Reconstructing Womanhood: The Emergence of the Afro-American Woman Novelist*. New York: Oxford UP, 1987.

Child, Lydia Maria. Introduction. *Incidents in the Life of a Slave Girl, Written by Herself*. By Harriet Jacobs. Cambridge: Harvard UP, 1987. 3–4.

Chopin, Kate. "The Story of an Hour." *A Vocation and a Voice: Stories*. Ed. Emily Toth. New York: Penguin, 1991. 76–79.

Christ, Carol P. *Diving Deep and Surfacing: Women Writers on Spiritual Quest*. Boston: Beacon, 1980.

Cooper, Anna Julia. *A Voice from the South*. 1892. New York: Oxford UP, 1988.

Cottom, Daniel. *The Civilized Imagination: A Study of Ann Radcliffe, Jane Austen, and Sir Walter Scott*. Cambridge: Cambridge UP, 1985.

Craft, Ellen and William. *Running a Thousand Miles for Freedom; or, The Escape of William and Ellen Craft from Slavery*. 1860. *Great Slave Narratives*. Ed. Arna Bontemps. Boston: Beacon, 1969.

Daly, Mary. *Gyn/Ecology: The Metaethics of Radical Feminism*. Boston: Beacon, 1978.

Darling, Marsha. "In the Realm of Responsibility: A Conversation with Toni Morrison." *Women's Review of Books* March 1988: 5–6.

Davis, Angela Y. *Women, Race and Class*. New York: Vintage, 1983.

Davis, David Brion. "Of Human Bondage." Rev. of *Slavery and Social Death* by Orlando Patterson. *New York Review of Books* 17 Feb. 1983: 19–22.

Day, William Patrick. *In the Circles of Fear and Desire: A Study of Gothic Fantasy*. Chicago: U of Chicago P, 1985.

"Declaration of Sentiments and Resolutions, Seneca Falls Convention, 1848." *Racism and Sexism: An Integrated Study*. Ed. Paula S. Rothenberg. New York: St. Martin's, 1988. 192–96.

DeLamotte, Eugenia C. *Perils of the Night: A Feminist Study of Nineteenth-Century Gothic*. New York: Oxford UP, 1990.

Dickinson, Emily. *The Poems of Emily Dickinson*. Ed. Thomas H. Johnson. Cambridge: Harvard UP, 1951.

Donaldson, Laura E. "The Miranda Complex: Colonialism and the Question of Feminist Reading." *Diacritics* 18.3 (1988): 65–77.

Douglass, Frederick. *Life and Times of Frederick Douglass.* 1892. New York: Collier-Macmillan, 1962.

———. *My Bondage and My Freedom.* 1855. Urbana: U of Illinois P, 1987.

———. *Narrative of the Life of Frederick Douglass, An American Slave, Written by Himself.* 1845. Cambridge: Harvard UP, 1960.

Drumgoold, Kate. *A Slave Girl's Story.* 1898. Gates, *Six Women's Slave Narratives.*

Du Bois, W. E. B. *The Souls of Black Folk.* 1903. New York: Bantam, 1989.

Eastman, Mary H. *Aunt Phillis's Cabin; or, Southern Life as It Is.* 1852. New York: Negro Universities P, 1960.

Elizabeth. "Memoir of Old Elizabeth, A Coloured Woman." 1863. Gates, *Six Women's Slave Narratives.*

Ellis, Kate Ferguson. *The Contested Castle: Gothic Novels and the Subversion of Domestic Ideology.* Urbana: U of Illinois P, 1989.

Fauset, Arthur Huff. *Sojourner, God's Faithful Pilgrim.* Chapel Hill: U of North Carolina P, 1938.

Fauset, Jessie Redmon. *Plum Bun: A Novel Without a Moral.* 1928. London: Pandora, 1985.

Fiedler, Leslie A. *Love and Death in the American Novel.* 1960. New York: Stein, 1966.

Fisher, Philip. *Hard Facts: Setting and Form in the American Novel.* New York: Oxford UP, 1985.

Fleenor, Juliann E., ed. *The Female Gothic.* Montreal: Eden, 1983.

Foucault, Michel. *The History of Sexuality.* Trans. Robert Hurley. New York: Vintage, 1980.

Fox-Genovese, Elizabeth. *Within the Plantation Household: Black and White Women of the Old South.* Chapel Hill: U of North Carolina P, 1988.

Franklin, H. Bruce. *The Victim as Criminal and Artist: Literature from the American Prison.* New York: Oxford UP, 1978.

Frye, Northrop. *Anatomy of Criticism.* Princeton: Princeton UP, 1957.

Fuller, Margaret. *Woman in the Nineteenth Century.* 1844. New York: Norton, 1971.

Furman, Marva J. "The Slave Narrative: Prototype of the Early Afro-American Novel." Sekora and Turner 120–26.

Gallagher, Catherine. *The Industrial Reformation of English Fiction: Social Discourse and Narrative Form, 1832–1867.* Chicago: U of Chicago P, 1985.

Gaskell, Elizabeth. *Life of Charlotte Brontë.* 1857. New York: Penguin, 1975.

Gates, Henry Louis, Jr. "Foreword: In Her Own Write." Gates, ed., *Six Women's Slave Narratives* vii–xxii.

———, ed. *Collected Black Women's Narratives.* New York: Oxford UP: 1988.

———. Introduction. *Our Nig.* By Harriet E. Wilson. New York: Random, 1983. xi–lix.

———, ed. *Six Women's Slave Narratives.* New York: Oxford UP, 1988.

————. "Writing 'Race' and the Difference It Makes." *Race, Writing, and Difference*. Chicago: U of Chicago P, 1986. 1–18.

Genovese, Eugene D. *Roll, Jordan, Roll: The World the Slaves Made*. New York: Vintage, 1976.

Gilbert, Sandra, and Susan Gubar. *The Madwoman in the Attic: The Woman Writer and the Nineteenth-Century Literary Imagination*. New Haven: Yale UP, 1979.

Gilman, Charlotte Perkins. *The Charlotte Perkins Gilman Reader: "The Yellow Wallpaper" and Other Fiction*. Ed. Ann J. Lane. New York: Pantheon, 1980.

Godwin, William. *Memoirs of Mary Wollstonecraft*. 1798. London: Constable, 1927.

Griffin, Susan. *Pornography and Silence: Culture's Revenge Against Nature*. New York: Harper, 1981.

Grimké, Angelina E. *Letters to Catharine E. Beecher, in Reply to an Essay on Slavery and Abolition, Addressed to A. E. Grimké*. Boston: Isaac Knapp, 1838.

Gwin, Minrose. *Black and White Women of the Old South: The Peculiar Sisterhood in American Literature*. Knoxville: U of Tennessee P, 1985.

Hawthorne, Nathaniel. *The House of the Seven Gables*. 1851. Norton Critical Ed. New York: Norton, 1967.

Hill, Bridget, ed. *The First English Feminist: Reflections upon Marriage and Other Writings by Mary Astell*. New York: St. Martin's, 1986.

Hirsch, Gordon. "The Monster Was a Lady: On the Psychology of Mary Shelley's *Frankenstein*." *Hartford Studies in Literature* 7 (1975): 116–53.

Hoagland, Sarah Lucia. *Lesbian Ethics: Toward New Value*. Palo Alto, Calif.: Institute of Lesbian Studies, 1988.

Homans, Margaret. *Bearing the Word: Language and Female Experience in Nineteenth-Century Women's Writing*. Chicago: U of Chicago P, 1986.

Hooks, Bell. *Ain't I a Woman: Black Women and Feminism*. Boston: South End, 1981.

Hurston, Zora Neale. *Their Eyes Were Watching God*. 1937. Urbana: U of Illinois P, 1978.

Jackson, Rosemary. *Fantasy: The Literature of Subversion*. London: Methuen, 1981.

Jacobs, Harriet A. *Incidents in the Life of a Slave Girl, Written by Herself*. 1861. Cambridge: Harvard UP, 1987.

Jaggar, Alison M. *Feminist Politics and Human Nature*. Totowa, N. J.: Rowman, 1983.

Jameson, Fredric. *The Political Unconscious: Narrative as a Socially Symbolic Act*. Ithaca: Cornell UP, 1981.

Johnson, James Weldon. *The Autobiography of an Ex-Colored Man*. 1912. New York: Penguin, 1990.

Kaplan, Cora. *Sea Changes: Culture and Feminism*. London: Verso, 1986.

Kauffman, Linda S. *Discourses of Desire: Gender, Genre, and Epistolary Fictions*. Ithaca: Cornell UP, 1986.

Kiely, Robert. *The Romantic Novel in England*. Cambridge: Harvard UP, 1972.

Kristeva, Julia. "Women's Time." *Signs* 7 (1981): 13–35.

Larsen, Nella. *"Quicksand" and "Passing."* 1928, 1929. New Brunswick: Rutgers UP, 1986.

Lee, Sophia. *The Recess*. 1783–85. New York: Arno, 1972.

Lewis, Matthew G. *The Monk*. 1796. New York: Grove, 1952.

Lorde, Audre. "The Transformation of Silence into Language and Action." *Sister Outsider: Essays and Speeches*. Freedom, Calif.: Crossing, 1984. 40–44.

Lovell, Terry. *Consuming Fiction*. London: Verso, 1987.

Mattison, Rev. H. "Louisa Picquet, The Octoroon: A Tale of Southern Slave Life." 1861. Gates, *Collected Black Women's Narratives*.

Maturin, Charles. *Melmoth the Wanderer*. 1820. New York: Penguin, 1984.

McDowell, Deborah E. "In the First Place: Making Frederick Douglass and the Afro-American Narrative Tradition." *Critical Essays on Frederick Douglass*. Ed. William L. Andrews. Boston: G. K. Hall, 1991. 192–214.

McIntyre, Clara Frances. *Ann Radcliffe in Relation to Her Time*. New Haven: Yale UP, 1920.

MacKethan, Lucinda H. "Metaphors of Mastery in the Slave Narratives." Sekora and Turner 55–69.

McKillop, Alan D. "Critical Realism in *Northanger Abbey*." *From Jane Austen to Joseph Conrad: Essays Collected in Memory of James T. Hillhouse*. Ed. Robert C. Rathburn and Martin Steinmann, Jr. Minneapolis: U of Minnesota P, 1958. 35–45.

Mellor, Anne K. *Mary Shelley: Her Life, Her Fiction, Her Monsters*. New York: Methuen, 1988.

———. "Possessing Nature: The Female in *Frankenstein*." *Romanticism and Feminism*. Ed. Anne K. Mellor. Bloomington: Indiana UP, 1988. 220–32.

Meyer, Susan L. "Colonialism and the Figurative Strategy of *Jane Eyre*." *Victorian Studies* 33 (1990): 247–68.

Mill, John Stuart. *The Subjection of Women*. 1869. Cambridge: MIT P, 1970.

Miller, Alice. *For Your Own Good: Hidden Cruelty in Child-Rearing and the Roots of Violence*. Trans. Hildegarde and Hunter Hannum. New York: Farrar, 1984.

———. *Thou Shalt Not Be Aware: Society's Betrayal of the Child*. Trans. Hildegarde and Hunter Hannum. New York: Meridian, 1986.

Mitchell, Juliet. *Psychoanalysis and Feminism: Freud, Reich, Laing, and Women*. New York: Vintage, 1975.

Modleski, Tania. *Loving with a Vengeance: Mass-Produced Fantasies for Women*. 1982. New York: Methuen, 1984.

Moers, Ellen. "Female Gothic." *Literary Women: The Great Writers*. New York: Doubleday, 1977.

Moi, Toril. *Sexual/Textual Politics: Feminist Literary Theory*. London: Methuen, 1985.

Morrison, Toni. *Beloved*. New York: Knopf, 1987.

———. "Unspeakable Things Unspoken: The Afro-American Presence in American Literature." *Michigan Quarterly Review* 28 (1989): 1–34.

Morrison, Toni, and Gloria Naylor. "A Conversation." *Southern Review* 21 (1985): 567–93.

Murray, E. B. *Ann Radcliffe.* New York: Twayne, 1972.

Napier, Elizabeth R. *The Failure of Gothic: Problems of Disjunction in an Eighteenth-Century Literary Form.* Oxford: Clarendon, 1987.

Nieboer, H. J. *Slavery as a Social System.* The Hague: Nijhoff, 1910.

Nisbet, Robert. "The Unfree." Rev. of *Slavery and Social Death* by Orlando Patterson. *Commentary* Apr. 1983: 74–76.

Nitchie, Elizabeth. Introduction. *Mathilda.* By Mary Shelley. Chapel Hill: U of North Carolina P, 1959. vii–xv.

Olsen, Tillie. *Silences.* New York: Delacorte, 1978.

Patterson, Orlando. *Slavery and Social Death: A Comparative Study.* Cambridge: Harvard UP, 1982.

Peters, Margot. *Unquiet Soul: A Biography of Charlotte Brontë.* 1975. New York: Atheneum, 1986.

Poe, Edgar Allan. *The Fall of the House of Usher and Other Writings.* New York: Penguin, 1986.

Poovey, Mary. "Ideology and *The Mysteries of Udolpho.*" *Criticism* 21 (1979): 307–30.

———. *The Proper Lady and the Woman Writer: Ideology as Style in the Works of Mary Wollstonecraft, Mary Shelley, and Jane Austen.* Chicago: U of Chicago P, 1984.

———. *Uneven Developments: The Ideological Work of Gender in Mid-Victorian England.* Chicago: U of Chicago P, 1988.

Praz, Mario. "Introductory Essay." *Three Gothic Novels.* New York: Penguin, 1968. 7–34.

———. *The Romantic Agony.* 1933. Trans. Angus Davidson. Cleveland: Meridian, 1968.

Prince, Mary. "The History of Mary Prince, A West Indian Slave." 1831. Gates, *Six Women's Slave Narratives.*

Prince, Nancy. "A Narrative of the Life and Travels of Mrs. Nancy Prince." 1853. Gates, *Collected Black Women's Narratives.*

Punter, David. *The Literature of Terror: A History of Gothic Fiction from 1765 to the Present Day.* London: Longman, 1980.

Quarles, Benjamin. Introduction. *Narrative of the Life of Frederick Douglass, An American Slave, Written by Himself.* By Frederick Douglass. Cambridge: Harvard UP, 1960. vii–xxvi.

Radcliffe, Ann. *The Italian; or, The Confessional of the Black Penitents, A Romance.* 1797. Oxford: Oxford UP, 1981.

———. *The Mysteries of Udolpho.* 1794. Oxford: Oxford UP, 1980.

———. "On the Supernatural in Poetry." *New Monthly Magazine and Literary*

Journal 16 (1826). "Original Papers," Part I. London: Henry Colburn, 1826. 145–52.

———. *The Romance of the Forest.* 1791. Oxford: Oxford UP, 1986.

Ragatz, Lowell Joseph. *The Fall of the Planter Class in the British Caribbean, 1763–1833: A Study in Social and Economic History.* New York: Century, 1928.

Restuccia, Frances L. "Female Gothic Writing: 'Under Cover to Alice.'" *Genre* 18 (1986): 245–66.

Retan, Katherine A. *Opening the Floodgates: The Construction of Gender and Class Boundaries in the Novels of Charlotte Brontë, Charles Dickens and Elizabeth Gaskell.* Diss. U of Minnesota, 1991. Ann Arbor: UMI, 1991. 9130189.

Rhys, Jean. *Wide Sargasso Sea.* 1966. New York: Norton, 1982.

Rich, Adrienne. "Compulsory Heterosexuality and Lesbian Existence." *Blood, Bread, and Poetry: Selected Prose, 1979–1985.* New York: Norton, 1986. 23–75.

———. "Jane Eyre: The Temptations of a Motherless Woman" and "Women and Honor: Some Notes on Lying." *On Lies, Secrets, and Silence: Selected Prose, 1966–1978.* New York: Norton, 1979. 89–106; 185–94.

———. *Of Woman Born: Motherhood as Experience and Institution.* New York: Bantam, 1976.

Rogers, Katharine M. *Feminism in Eighteenth-Century England.* Urbana: U of Illinois P, 1982.

Russ, Joanna. *How to Suppress Women's Writing.* Austin: U of Texas P, 1983.

———. "Somebody's Trying to Kill Me and I Think It's My Husband: The Modern Gothic." Fleenor 31–56.

Sadleir, Michael. "The Northanger Novels: A Footnote to Jane Austen." English Pamphlet 68. London: Oxford UP, 1927.

Sanger, Charles Percy. "The Structure of *Wuthering Heights.*" *Wuthering Heights.* By Emily Brontë. 2nd Norton Critical Edition. New York: Norton, 1972. 286–98.

Sedgwick, Eve Kosofsky. *The Coherence of Gothic Conventions.* New York: Methuen, 1986.

Sekora, John. "Black Message/White Envelope: Genre, Authenticity, and Authority in the Antebellum Slave Narrative." *Callaloo* 32 (1987): 482–515.

———. *Luxury: The Concept in Western Thought, Eden to Smollett.* Baltimore: Johns Hopkins UP, 1977.

Sekora, John, and Houston A. Baker, Jr. "Written Off: Narratives, Master Texts, and Afro-American Writing from 1760 to 1945." *Studies in Black American Literature.* Vol. 1. Ed. Joe Weixlmann and Chester J. Fontenot. Greenwood, Fla.: Penkevill, 1984. 43–62.

Sekora, John, and Darwin T. Turner, eds. *The Art of Slave Narrative: Original Essays in Criticism and Theory.* Macomb: Western Illinois UP, 1982.

Shelley, Mary. *Frankenstein; or, The Modern Prometheus.* 1818, 1831. New York: Penguin, 1985.

———. *The Letters of Mary Wollstonecraft Shelley.* Ed. Betty T. Bennett. 3 vols. Baltimore: Johns Hopkins UP, 1980–88.

———. *Mary Shelley's Journal.* Ed. Frederick L. Jones. Norman: U of Oklahoma P, 1947.

———. *Mathilda.* Chapel Hill: U of North Carolina P, 1959.

Smith, James McCune. Introduction. *My Bondage and My Freedom.* By Frederick Douglass. Urbana: U of Illinois P, 1987. 9–23.

Smith, Valerie. *Self-Discovery and Authority in Afro-American Narrative.* Cambridge: Harvard UP, 1987.

Spencer, Jane. *The Rise of the Woman Novelist: From Aphra Behn to Jane Austen.* Oxford: Blackwell, 1986.

Spender, Dale. *Mothers of the Novel: One Hundred Good Women Writers Before Jane Austen.* London: Pandora, 1986.

Spillers, Hortense J. "Mama's Baby, Papa's Maybe: An American Grammar Book." *Diacritics* 17 (1987): 65–81.

Spivak, Gayatri Chakravorty. "Three Women's Texts and a Critique of Imperialism." *"Race," Writing, and Difference.* Ed. Henry Louis Gates, Jr. Chicago: U of Chicago P, 1986. 262–80.

Stepto, Robert B. *From Behind the Veil: A Study of Afro-American Narrative.* Urbana: U of Illinois P, 1979.

Sterling, Dorothy, ed. *We Are Your Sisters: Black Women in the Nineteenth Century.* New York: Norton, 1984.

Stowe, Harriet Beecher. *Uncle Tom's Cabin.* 1852. New York: Harper, 1965.

Sunstein, Emily. *Mary Shelley: Romance and Reality.* Boston: Little, 1989.

Tillotson, Marcia. "'A Forced Solitude': Mary Shelley and the Creation of Frankenstein's Monster." Fleenor 167–75.

Todorov, Tzvetan. *The Fantastic: A Structural Approach to a Literary Genre.* Trans. Richard Howard. Cleveland: P of Case Western Reserve U, 1973.

Tompkins, J. M. S. *The Popular Novel in England, 1770–1800.* London: Methuen, 1932.

Walker, Alice. *The Color Purple.* New York: Pocket, 1982.

Walpole, Horace. *The Castle of Otranto.* 1765. New York: Penguin, 1968.

White, Deborah Grey. *Ar'n't I a Woman? Female Slaves in the Plantation South.* New York: Norton, 1985.

Williams, Raymond. *The English Novel: From Dickens to Lawrence.* London: Hogarth, 1984.

Wilson, Harriet E. *Our Nig; or, Sketches from the Life of a Free Black, In a Two-Story White House, North: Showing that Slavery's Shadows Fall Even There.* 1859. New York: Random, 1983.

Wise, T. J., and J. A. Symington, eds. *The Brontës: Their Lives, Friendships and Correspondence.* 4 vols. Oxford: Shakespeare Head P, 1932.

Wollstonecraft, Mary. *Mary, A Fiction and Maria; or, The Wrongs of Woman.* Ed. Gary Kelly. London: Oxford UP, 1976.

————. *A Vindication of the Rights of Woman.* 1792. 2nd ed. New York: Norton, 1988.

Woolf, Virginia. *A Room of One's Own.* 1929. New York: Harcourt, 1957.

Yellin, Jean Fagan. Introduction. *Incidents in the Life of a Slave Girl, Written by Herself.* By Harriet A. Jacobs. Cambridge: Harvard UP, 1987. xiii–xxxiv.

————. *Women and Sisters: The Antislavery Feminists in American Culture.* New Haven: Yale UP, 1989.

INDEX